William M Allen

Five Years in the West

Or, how an inexperienced young man finds his occupation

William M Allen

Five Years in the West
Or, how an inexperienced young man finds his occupation

ISBN/EAN: 9783337426569

Printed in Europe, USA, Canada, Australia, Japan

Cover: Foto ©Andreas Hilbeck / pixelio.de

More available books at **www.hansebooks.com**

FIVE YEARS IN THE WEST;

OR,

How an Inexperienced Young Man Finds His Occupation.

WITH

Reminiscences and Sketches of Real Life.

By a Texas Preacher

NASHVILLE, TENN.:
SOUTHERN METHODIST PUBLISHING HOUSE.
1884.

PUBLISHED

IN THE INTEREST OF

THE SOUTH-WESTERN UNIVERSITY.

Entered, according to Act of Congress, in the year 1884,
BY WILLIAM ALLEN,
in the Office of the Librarian of Congress, at Washington.

PREFACE.

THIS volume is small, and will therefore take but an evening of precious time to peruse it. Let it have but a fair chance, and then approve or condemn, as is right. It is given to the public as truth, and not as fiction. Take the disguise out of it, and much of it could be established by living witnesses.

The plan adopted is this: The author had been in the West from the time he was verging into manhood, but after a number of years returned to visit his mother. She requested him to give a narrative of his life and experience in the West. This little volume is the narrative as he related it to her. An understanding of this plan is necessary to proper appreciation.

THE AUTHOR.

JULY 12, 1883.

TO THE MEMORY OF MY MOTHER,

WHOSE VIRTUOUS TRAINING HAS INFLUENCED MY FOOT-

STEPS THROUGH ALL THE CHANGING

FORTUNES OF MY LIFE.

THE AUTHOR.

CONTENTS.

	PAGE
A Visit Back—Not the Old Homestead—The Meeting—Questions.	11
Mother's Answer—Request	14
Beginning of the Narration—Heroism of Leaving Home	17
The Novelty in Things to an Inexperienced Boy	19
Loneliness and its Effect—Courage	20
Views of Mankind as a Herd	21
Old Letters Brought to Light	22
Letter on Kansas's Political State	23
Remarks	25
Letter on Indian Life and Character	27
Remarks	29
In Texas—At a Loss—Discouragements	30
Green from the States—Want of Experience	31
My First Speculation—Land Certificates—Fraud	33
Turned Pedagogue—Whisky	34
The Acquaintance and History of Two Young Doctors	36
How Innocency is Taken Out of the Human Heart	38
A Scene on the Square Around my Court-house School-room	39
About Dancing	41
A Plan to Regain my Lost Fortune	45
How I Made Atonement for Being a Partisan	47
Disgust—Musings—Looking to the Legal Profession	48
Finding at Last my Proper Life Business	51
Letters on the Ministry to my Mother	55
Mother's Reply	57
Reflections on a Call to the Ministry	59
The Troubles and Embarrassments of Starting	60

CONTENTS.

	PAGE
My First Sermon	62
Going to my First Conference	64
At Conference—A Sketch	68
In the Conference-room	71
The Outlook Among the Brethren	72
Reading the Appointments	73
My Assignment—Sorrow—Incidents	74
The Surprise of the Night	77
My Bereaved Sister	79
Horse Swapping	81
How I Finally Got Mounted for the Mission Work	84
On the Missions—My New Title	86
My First Sermon on the Missions—Singing—"Brother Jesse"—Frontier Meeting-house	87
The Evening Service and the Fruits it Bore	89
Area of the Missions—Meeting with the Senior Preacher	92
Character of the People	93
Expectation Blasted—Disgust	94
Buncombe County Illustrated—Further Comment	97
Brother Jones Again—My Lesson from Sister Jones	101
An Illustrative Anecdote	106
A Portion of Country Described	107
Coffee—How I Remedied an Evil	108
Meeting with an Old Greek Grammar	110
Descriptions—Master Payton	111
Preaching in a Frontier Dwelling-house—How the People go to Preaching on the Frontier	118
Leave Hamilton's for the West Fork of the Trinity River—Luck of the Night	120
The Evil of Dancing	127
Snuffing the War-breeze	130
Meeting with Universalism	132
The Recount	136
An Old Lady who had seen Better Days	137

CONTENTS.

	PAGE
Isaiah xxviii. 20	139
The Unlucky Night	141
The Cyclone	144
On an Indian Trail	148
The Brother who was Going to Make me a Nice Present	151
Out and In the Compass of the Gospel	155
The Tongue—James iii. 3–8	157
Necessity the Mother of Invention	160
A Singular Phenomenon	163
Mischievous Turn to Call the People Out	166
The Strait of the Young Preacher in Administering a Reproof	169
The Stiff Preacher	172
How the Young Preacher got Cheated out of a Sermon	173
Some Disadvantages	177
The Ungoverned Family	179
Dismissing the Missions, etc.	184
Advice of an Old Preacher—Going to Conference Again	189
At Conference Again	191
Reading the Appointments	193
Thoughts—Rest—Start for the Station	195
Observations on the Way	197
Impressions of the Place	199
First Sermon in the Station	201
Fishing and Fishers	202
Hon. William L. Yancey	205
Anchored in a Lake	207
My Last Days in the Station	210

FIVE YEARS IN THE WEST.

A Visit Back—Not the Old Homestead—The Meeting—Questions.

WELL, here I am after a long absence; not, however, among the oaks and walnuts of the old homestead, yet, nevertheless, in a place pleasant enough—even in the presence of her to whom I owe a debt of gratitude I shall never be able to pay. Why, here in this beech-forest on Kentucky's soil, and on the banks of Green River, is a pleasant place; yet I see none of the traces of the old homestead outlined here. I do not see the brook in whose clayey bank I used to dig my springs, build my dams, and erect my corn-stalk flutter-mills. I do not see the old apple-orchard in which I passed so many frolicksome days, and in which the cat-bird sung for me at early morn. A thousand things are missing here, but *one* is present who more than compensates for them all. And well do I remember now that not for the sake of oak and walnuts, not for the old brook with its clayey banks, springs, and mills, not for the song of cat-birds at early morn, not for the solitudinous note of the whip-poor-will in dusky eve, have I returned from the far West. No; I came with a mind more appreciative and an affection more dear. I came to see again the face of her who gave me birth; to press again those hands that did so fondly caress me in the innocency of my cradle-life; to press tenderly, with true filial affection, a kiss once more on those lovely lips now growing thinner and more tremulous with age.

Time works his changes. This is another homestead, yet it has a fragrance sweet. It is a spot most dear and sacred. Mother, is that you standing at the door waiting and anxiously looking for your long absent son. Yes, I know you now. I saw you take a step. It was a limping one. I understand it, for I remember well, long years ago, when on returning from church, whither to go was your delight, a fall from your horse laid the foundation for that limping gait. And you can remember how by your side I held you fast when mounted again, and how with slow pace we at last gained our cottage home. Many a pain went through my young heart then, while trudging along I looked up into your pale face and read your sufferings in blue, quivering lips.

Driver, halt! Let me leave your conveyance and reverently afoot approach the form I see meeting me yonder. Mother, these caresses are not signs of mental weakness either in thee or myself. They are but miniature outcroppings of that godly nature remaining yet in our race, and not left behind in Eden's bower when man was driven out in transgression. I see thy form now a little bent, and thy face more marked by the ravages of time; thy voice now not so full in tone as once it was; but on thy brow I read more than the serenity and calm resignation of other years. When I balance all things, I cannot say that thou hast lost more than thou hast gained. These ravages of time marked on thy face are not abrupt and angular, but rest in beautiful curving lines. These are just such as God loves, for even the revolving spheres under his appointment do make continually curving circuits. There is a background in thy expression which time has never touched. It touches in me the same chord that keeps yet alive my youthful admiration. I find thee now as beautifully fair as when sixteen years ago I left our old hearth-stone to try my fortunes in the far West, and among strangers.

But come now, tell me, have you not been thinking I had forgotten you? Have you not lost pleasure and passed hours in sadness by my long absence? Were those others I left behind with you enough for your comfort? or would you in the twilight of the evening catch yourself looking toward the West thinking of me? Did you see a vacant chair around the old hearth-stone when in the shades of the evening the family circle was formed, and each tyro for himself, before taking up books and papers, narrated the battle of the day? When the merry laugh went round, would the silence at my old chair show that joy could have been more complete? Did brothers and sisters often mention my name? Did they often go and get the picture I left behind, and with cherished memory talk of me? Did you ever observe marked attention in the younger ones when on occasion you would narrate to them some of the incidents and early battles of my life? Above all, before I left for the West had you discovered principles in me worthy to be cherished, which you could call on the younger ones to emulate, and for the sake of which your soul could rest in hope?

Mother's Answer—Request.

"My dear boy"—this is my old familiar style, and it is to-day fresh and green in my memory—"your questions remind me of earlier days when I was a young and happy mother; not that I am unhappy now, but different from those days, for my little boys were around me then. Those days, I might say, were my happiest. Questions then, as from you now, fell thick and fast from the lips of my little boys. Though I did my best to satisfy every inquiring mind, yet the ingenuity of sharp little wits taxed my understanding to a degree that I waived many a question through the business of the day.

"But let me say, my dear son, you know not the depth of a mother's love. It is of its own kind, and peculiarly devoted to its object. Its existence brings up not only the memory of the object, but holds, as painted on canvas, the image of the one she fondly cherishes. It is but a speck of that godly nature acquired in her high origin, and left her yet on this stormy and wave-dashed beach, not alone for her own comfort, but to use as a means of giving the best character to her offspring. To disrobe her nature of an element so embellishing, so noble, would be to leave her little urchin boy-plant to be bruised and battered by the rough winds of sin. It would lay the foundation of the future man in the sloughs and baser elements of a sinful nature, and undermine the refinement and moral bearing of society. It would open the flood-gates of vice, and send a corrupting, blighting tidal-wave of moral ruin that in aspect would make earth the counterpart of the world of woe. If the intellectual and moral elevation of the human race is attributable to one thing especially above all other earthly things, it is this God-given heritage—a mother's love. This is the spring that moves her to protect her helpless offspring. Yet this is the least view of it. The grandest field of its operation consists in looking into and providing for the proper manhood life of the little boy at her knee. Hence, if she is properly educated, or if her thoughts run in the proper channel, she studies and untiringly labors to build in him a foundation of integrity and true morality.

"A mother's love is not abated by space or the lapse of time. The instinctive races, or lower animals, that have minds which cater to mere animal wants—that are incapable of rising above appetite and selfishness, that lack a moral crown, the requisite of an accountable being—may and do forget their offspring after they are weaned away; but a mother's love for her darling boy burns with a glow of unabated interest through life. It is one of those attributes of her spiritual nature which can never die.

"Again, I have had many occasions of observing a kindred element in the breasts of sisters and brothers you left behind with me. Often in my own young days I have felt the affection that naturally exists between brothers and sister; but I have learned more of this principle from observation than from personal experience. I have often observed on wintry night, when the winds howled wildly round, yet all whom you left behind comfortably encircling the old hearth-stone—lulled to silence by their own meditations, apparently thinking of the burning wood or the glowing coal—there would be a thought reaching far beyond this scene; for just on such an occasion some one would ask of the brother now gone to the West. Then would come up anew the incidents of his life. No; your name, my dear boy, was not forgotten by the fond ones left behind. It was cherished by brothers and sisters, and fondly remembered by a loving mother. The books you loved most were handled and talked of; the anecdotes you used to tell and tales you narrated were repeated.

"We cherished no thought that you had forgotten us and home. We felt that the sacredness of the spot was too dear, and the tie of kindred too strong, to indulge such an illusion. Home, home—we felt there was no place like home. Your letters breathed this spirit. We felt that we could more easily forget you than that you could forget us; yet we knew we could not forget you.

"But, come now, son, tell me something of the struggle you had in parting with us and in saying farewell. Tell me of the times you have had in the West. Surely now, by this time—a life varied as yours has been—you have made a little sketch of history to which I can listen with much interest. You have written us some things, yet there appears to be about you a novelty that makes us anxious to hear."

Beginning of the Narration—Heroism of Leaving Home.

"Mother, I fear to answer your questions will prove to you a fatiguing task, and tax your patience. If I should tell it all, the sun would sink to rest more than once before my voice would be hushed in rest, having found an end to my thoughts on life's battle and what it is. I shall only take up those parts which I think will interest you most, and on which you can exercise patience. At your request I will begin; nevertheless, if you grow weary before I have reached the end, I pray you give me a token, and I will postpone my train of thought till another day. You are growing old now, and should have your proper rest; yet I remember when I was young in years, and had not yet engaged in life's big battle, you oft entertained us of evenings until the hour was late, and yet we never wearied as long as we could hear you talk. And while I hear you say those were among your happiest days, I say they would have been happy days indeed for me were it not for that delusive fancy in a boy that looks for true happiness only in the bearded man. This delusion, I suppose, will continue to exist, since the art which will take this conceit out of a boy, if ever known, is lost.

"The heroism of my life appears to me to be more striking now than during the changing events of its history. How I found courage to leave the family, and especially a mother whom I cherished in memory with the fondest affection, when my nature seemed to revolt at the idea, is a problem not easily solved. I do not mean how some other boy merging into manhood could leave home; for, doubtless, many a boy lives whose home environments would bring relief when broken; but, knowing my own experience, when it choked my utterance, and seemed to break the currents of my flowing blood—when it seemed to be a revolution unnatural, tearing as it were flesh from flesh and heart from heart—I repeat, I have ever looked on it since as a problem in my own mind. But having obtained my own consent to go, leave home with all its fond endearments, and seek my fortune of life in the West, I resolved to fight the battle through. It was the first hard battle of my life. It was a struggle I have never desired to repeat. To this day, it gives me no pleasure to think of it; yet it is a part, even the beginning, of my independent history, and I have repeated the story of it to you because it comes first in this narration, and is therefore in order here. If I should recount all the battles of my life, and count out one that used me worst, this is the one I would select. It is not that my life has been without other battles, but it is by comparison to show the magnitude of this. You know how I gave the parting hand, though you never knew the struggle in my heart, and had it not been I am a son of thine I could never have displayed such moral heroism."

The Novelty in Things to an Inexperienced Boy.

"But the scene of bidding adieu to loved ones, and leaving home, sweet home, became a thing of the past, as all things do, and I got fairly on my way. The gap between home and myself got wider and wider as the days passed by. Many things new to me now appeared, and my young mind feasted on these. Every thing had a freshness and novelty to me, whose experience had never reached but a few miles beyond the borders of home-life. The novelty of the things I saw, all new to me—the rivers, steamboats, railroads, cities with their din and business bustle, natural scenery, the beautiful and the sublime—gave me pleasure indescribable, and in some degree abated my thoughts of home, sweet home, and the loved ones there. In gradual turn, as I suppose, my face now began to grow bright again. While I indulged in thoughts of home with rapturous joy, I found that pleasures may arise from other sources than from home, sweet home. More than a thousand miles now had I traversed in saddle. The grand expanse of the West began to open on my vision. The world to me began to look larger. My vision was no longer checked as on Kentucky's soil, where the trees grow thick and tall, and where the hills are both short and steep; but sweeping over high-rolling prairies with their long slopes, vision here is only brought to an end by the distant blue, dusky hue of sunset. Yet I thought if you could see only one sunset in the wilds of the West, it would be to you a charming vision.

"But expansive views and natural scenery are not

all that attracted my young mind then. The prairie abounds with inhabitants peculiarly its own; the deer and antelope in herds by scores; wild horses in herds here and there; buffalo in large herds spot the prairie dark like islands on the sea, or grazing in long dark lines, destroy the monotony of vision; the long-eared hare or buck-rabbit, or as the boys call it mule-ear, whose fleetness, when in health, is yet unknown; the stinging scorpion with vertebrated tail, whose favorite resort is under old rails and rocks, and whose most cultivated business is to warn you of his presence with most unpleasant sensations when you put your fingers just far enough under to turn the rail or raise the rock; the prairie dog whose chief companions are owls and rattlesnakes—with them is great concord, although the young *marmot* is a dainty morsel to either. And yet again, there are to be found the horned frog, which is rather a misnomer for lizard, as is plainly indicated both by its form and mode of traveling; the tarantula, or big spider, usually of slow, clumsy motion, which carries its fangs carefully folded underneath its body, and which are a quarter of an inch long; the centipede, that repulsive, crusty-looking creature, rightly named as far as the word goes, with every foot like a poisonous fang—a reptile that loves droughty weather and cracks in the ground."

Loneliness and its Effect—Courage.

"But I must tell you that on many a night I felt the deep stillness of the solitude creep over me. Oppressing gloom would sometimes shadow me around, so that I could not suppress the rising spirit of deep loneliness. Often then would I wish for sleep, for a night's rest always made me feel better. The solitude of the night, however, when among strangers, brought me no alarm; it only haunted me with the thought that this is not home. There was no sound of brother, no voice of a sister, no consoling presence of mother. The landscapes, forests, and wide, wide prairies, mapped on my vision, were all different to the old homestead and the scenery around. I love solitude sometimes, especially when the circumstances of my life give me only a short ramble through its gloom.

"If I had indulged the thought, when weighed down by feelings of loneliness, that on the morrow I will direct my steed toward the East, I will give up other views of the West, I will seek my fortune of life around the old homestead, where I love its orchard, meadows, and the shades of its locust-trees, then rest would have come uninvited, and sleep would have been balmy and refreshing. But this I could not do. I was full of a genuinely proud spirit. This is a heritage you gave me. I was not born a coward. I could not entertain a thought of abusing my noble heritage. I was, as I realized, out in the heat of life's battle, and I determined to play a part becoming a true soldier."

Views of Mankind as a Herd.

"The world, I found, was not as cold, selfish, and taciturn as I had suspected. Among men may be found the counterpart of the serpent, dog, hog, wolf, fox, or bear. But these are exceptions to the general rule. They may in the main be avoided. Notwithstanding the complete ruin of the human heart by original transgression, the impressive force of Christianity, both in the direct operation of the Spirit on man's nature and in forming the manners of society, the herd of mankind have much of kindness and sympathy. These, however, do not stand out prominently to the view. They exist in a latent state, but are excited into action on all proper occasions. The judgment of the world is that the traveler should be a gentleman. When he satisfies this judgment, he never wants for friends. There is a class of men whose hands are against every other man. All other men, as well as the traveler, are in danger from these. They are the wolf-fiends and prowling Bedouins—the curses to society, who with dark hearts, ruined moral natures, laboring under false ideas, set up the claim that the world owes them a living without work; and all this contrary to the revealed decree that man shall 'eat his bread in the sweat of his face.'"

Old Letters Brought to Light.

"If I remember rightly, I wrote you some letters on Kansas troubles, and then again some on Indian life and manners. Have they been given to the waste-basket? or are they now on file somewhere? Not that they have merit or deserve immortality, do I ask; but by interluding a letter or two, lying as they do in the track of my narrative, it will, if they are read by some one else, give me a respite, after which I promise you I will try and be more entertaining. I used to keep my budget of compositions, my early literary triumphs, deep down in the old historic clock, which used to stand from floor to floor—a length prodigious in comparison with clocks now. But I do not see that long-time machine around anywhere. When I left, that budget was laid away carefully there. At some future time I may ask of that budget and of that clock, which was the great curiosity of my early boyhood.

"Yes, here is a budget of letters you have carefully kept. They contain incidents of my travels with my young attempts to philosophize on men and things. Thanks to you, brother Fielding, for looking them up. Why, they look a little musty now! It is the way they show their age. Every thing has its own way of telling how it has left the years behind. I observe when looking in a glass that time has marked the lines he intends to plow in my own face. Every year he intends to run the same lines, and every time he plows leave the furrows more distinctly marked. Why, these pages are sixteen years old! Then, time has plowed them sixteen times. This is enough to give them that dusky look they bear. But let us hear some of them read. Brother Fielding will please perform the pleasant task:

LEAVENWORTH, KANSAS, November, '56.

My Dear Mother and Loved Ones at Home: I am here at an exciting season, and in the midst of an excited people. Kansas is not a pleasant country; not even to the politically unconcerned. Every resident here is compelled to be a partisan. To be neutral is the worst course a citizen can take. He is then absolutely out of respect, and subject to the abuse of both free-soilers and pro-slavery men. He must be something; for if manhood is in him, he evidently is something, and his surroundings compel him to let it out. It is sad to think of the political stew in this territory. I verily believe the spirit of party has gone fanatically wild out here. I regard that as the disease, and not an honest, virtuous concern for the negro. It is this that will yet ruin the nation.

A man is happy out here prospectively. All depends on the result of elections. There is but little honesty in these. The *furor* raging here indulges any thing that will secure success. The greatest man is he who is successful without counting modes. In the equal division of the parties, I shall count those the biggest rogues who carry it as a State.

There is a sort of intuitive knowledge here of a man's politics. A man here is seldom asked for his politics, but is conversed with as though he is perfectly understood on these points. They locate the State of a man by his dress mainly, and in this they seldom make mistakes. When once the State of an immigrant or a traveler is located, he is approached as a Southern or Northern man in his political philosophy according to the political nature of the State from which he came. True, some of the States are considerably divided in political creed, yet the nature of immigration to this territory is of a kind that has very seldom brought Northern ideas from Southern States or Southern ideas from Northern States. I pass here as a Kentuckian; yet no one asks me, and yet again everybody regards me of pro-slavery principle. This all comes of the mixed suit you prepared me, and which I find pleasure in wearing out here. In politics they go here by States. That is the rule. There are a few exceptions. But woe to the poor fellow who stands an exception to the rule! It would have been better for him if he had never come out here. He is poor and friendless, and regarded as a traitor by one party, and lacks the confidence of the other.

This territory, so far as I have seen, has a beautiful face. In its physical aspect it is as beautiful as one should desire. It has a probable future of wonderful growth in wealth and population. But it has a present imbittered by strife, and a population divided and full of treachery toward each other. I shall not remain here many days. Every thing seems to be on a war footing. Every day brings a history of revenge, burning, bloodshed, and suffering. The hate that lurks in many hearts here makes this a very unsafe country. They do many things here under the rule of *lex talionis*, which you know is both rude and uncivilized. Here in miniature form is playing that which is inevitably coming on us as a nation, unless the question of slavery is solidly settled. Would to God the authorities of the nation could see the rising storm, and drive back its force before it bursts with dread and maddening fury through all the States, and to the sorrow of many a heart.

Your affectionate son, ...

REMARKS.

"This is a picture of Kansas's political state as it existed then, described as well as I could tell it now. While traveling there, the *débris* of many a house I saw, such as the fire would leave—many a family homeless and destitute. Here the battle between the States began; for nearly all the States were represented in the contest that went on here. It was only an armistice from this time till '61. It was a smoldering, suppressed calm, awaiting the storm-clouds to gather more furiously, and the thunder-heads of war to grow large, that when they burst every dog of war might howl in echo until the drapery of sorrow about every hearthstone should show the nation's gloom. The storm came, and blew in hate, blood, and murder till all fools satisfied their thirst—till it was thought better to be governed by reason than by passion.

"But let us walk lightly among these dark shadows of the past. I hardly need mention the cold, malicious murder of Uncle John—that affable Christian gentleman, your own brother—by the hands of those who should have been his friends; nor my nephew, and others who fell on Shiloh's field; nor another, who was dearer both to you and me. No, I need not mention these; for I see the war-wind bearing on you now in these days when your burden should be light. Once you owned servants whom you used kindly; I see none around you now. They are gone with the freedom they acquired through the strife. For these you received no compensation to enable you to procure the necessary help you need now in the decrepitude of age. That property you acquired through the sweat of your face, honestly, and under the protected law of the government. It is too much the fashion of governments to claim exemptions through war measures. This, however, cannot strengthen them; for such a policy as was adopted toward the South, instead of cementing the people as a whole, tended rather to alienate their affection.

"A lost cause often carries down with it many just claims which ought to have been respected. How the nation shall atone for many of its deeds, and when the atonement shall be made, are questions locked up in the mysterious future, and known only unto God. Atonements are sometimes made in the moral government of God when the primal causes that produced them have gone out of the memory of man. Small seeds, working through generations, after awhile often bring wonderful developments, operating as they do powerfully upon the reason of man.

"But let these sad memories go to oblivion. Let us train our minds to look on the sunny side of things, for there is where our pleasure lies. Let us commit these things to the all-wise Ruler of the universe, who can bring good out of evil, and who, when let alone, doeth all things well.

"I fear, dear mother, my digression has not been as interesting as my narrative; yet it seemed naturally to grow out of the letter which has just been read. But here is another letter, on another subject, with sentiment as pure as my young perception could make it:

CULBERT FERRY, RED RIVER, TEXAS LINE, December, '56.

Dear Mother and Loved Ones at Home: I am now at the entrance to Texas. I have seen much more, which remains yet untold, than I can write you in one letter. I think I could now, if present with you, enliven the old family circle until a late hour with the stories and reminiscences of my travels. I will tell you in this only about the Indians. I am now leaving their territory, though I am not weary. I would like to remain awhile yet with them, the better to learn their manners. Let me see, I have now been through the Delawares, Shawnees, Pottawattamies, Senecas, Cherokees, Creeks, Chickasaws, and Choctaws. What a list of names, some of you think; yet these are only a few of the many when we come to a general summing up of all the tribes. I believe these, however, are the most cultivated of all the American Indians; yet their civilization is very small in comparison with the opportunities they have had. To evolve a genuine type of the civilian out of the red man will require a long period of time. The problem has to be added, subtracted, multiplied, and divided through several generations.

They are constitutionally opposed to civilization. They embrace the philosophy, in its most emphatic sense, that the spontaneity of the earth answers every end of substance and happiness. They have no inclination to fell forests or till the soil; to bridge rivers, build cities, and other industries. They think these torment the brain and torture the body unnecessarily, and therefore tend to destroy that spontaneity which gives ease and comfort.

I have no doubt that the advantages and treachery of the whites impeded their progress in civilization by destroying their confidence. If every man who treated with or administered to the Indians had been a Penn or an Eliot, they would have had more confidence in the white race. Their progress in civilization and religion would consequently have been more rapid. As it is, their competition with the white race will ultimate in little else than extinction.

I think the history they have made is worth preserving. If some one would dwell with these forest tribes awhile, and gather up their unwritten history as they hold it in tradition, I think it would make an exceedingly entertaining book. Their virtues have never been written. United States history is prejudiced against them. They are known to be a treacherous people, it is true; but when they tell their own history the white race have nothing praiseworthy or that merits a boast in the comparison.

It is strange to relate, yet some of these people have become wealthy —only just a few. They own slaves just the same as the whites. Some few, after so long a time, have opened farms, give considerable attention to agriculture, and consequently have plenty around them. But as a rule they have the same rudeness in dress, and live by hunting and fishing, as when America was first discovered.

Reticence is a marked feature in their character. They have been careless about learning English. I found a few who were pretty well educated, having attended our colleges. These are free to converse; yet even they take no pleasure in dwelling on the history of the tribes. On this subject they have little to say to the stranger. You may learn more of their history from the orations of Red Jacket, Logan, and Osceola than as a stranger holding converse. Their reticence on the subject of their history, however, abates as the newness of the stranger grows old.

Travelers are sometimes at a loss to find their way when traveling among these tribes for want of some English-speaking one. Should their eyes, however, fall on one of those sable sons of Africa, they need never fear. They can all speak English, and love it with a relish. They are a most accommodating people toward the traveler, and in affability try to show themselves superior to their red masters. They do not appear to be unhappy. Some of them told me of the life they once lived among the whites. Some came with their white masters, who concluded to live with the Indians; some were bought. They are all kindly treated.

The native religion of these tribes, if they have any, is hard to find. They have a notion of a Great Spirit, at the head of both the physical and moral universe, who will see that ample provision is made in the future for all good Indians. They seem to lose sight of bad Indians at death, and do not indulge in any dreamy speculations about their fate. They seem to forget such. They say nothing about them.

Their code of morals and civil jurisprudence is that Indians should do right—love their friends, hate their enemies, cherish friendly deeds, and revenge wrongs. Outside of missionary operations, they have no public demonstrations in religion, no religious harangues, and of course no prayers, no churches. They give their consent to the Great Spirit. Their good actions all come out of this consent through the monitor within them. They live and die in faith, without doubting. When I come to Kentucky I will give you some sketches of personal experience with these red men.

Your affectionate son, ---------------------

REMARKS.

"I am truly glad these letters have been preserved. These sketches of the subjects to which they pertain speak my present convictions. They seem not to have been written with the excitement through the novelty of things that sometimes gives color to the truth. Now, by your cheery looks you seem not to have grown weary, though I feared the reading would tax your patience, since these letters I have found here on file long since have been enjoyed by you and carefully stored away. I am glad you enjoyed the reading so much. I reckon it is because your long absent son has returned; or, if not, because they date a period of time near when your little boys were around your knee, could prattle, caper round in yard and orchard, which you say were among your most joyful days. And now methinks for these and other reasons you found a leisure hour to now and then read these and other letters I wrote you when far away. Then I am glad I wrote them, for it makes me happy to know you found pleasure in them. But now I will unwind my ball, or pick up my thread—not, however, like Theseus, the athlete, to enter a labyrinth, slay a dreaded beast, and by my thread find egress again. No, I have done no marvelous deed like that. Yet I trust I have spun a thread of life that will at least bring no pang to my heart nor yours while I follow the thread and put life under review again."

In Texas—At a Loss—Discouragements.

I found myself at last on Texas soil. Not in the pine-wood district of the eastern portion, but in the expansive prairie region, favorable for large views, not only of the eye, but also of the mind. Here I felt that I was more out on an ocean sailing than at any period since I left "home, sweet home." I resolved to make Texas the State of my adoption. I might have remained in Kansas but for the political agitation in that territory, and, as I regarded, uncertainty in all things. What to do I knew not, yet do something I must. I felt in me all the awkwardness of an inexperienced young man thrust out among strangers to learn a business or profession. Many a boy in the West, when all alone, right here has stumbled in the deliriousness of his own meditations. Many a man with his family around him, under similar circumstances has suffered such confusion that he retraced his steps, broken in fortune, to be among the same hills and beside the same brook he left awhile before.

Such is life—the stream ebbs and flows, fortunes are sought and made; yet men go down the hill jolting and thumping, unable to check their course, wondering at every rock and acclivity why they started and whither they are going, until want echoes round that they have reached the broad plain from which all beginnings start.

GREEN FROM THE STATES—WANT OF EXPERIENCE.

I realized the fact that was more than once sounded in my ears—that I was "*green from the States.*" Everybody seemed to know more than I did—even the cowboys, whose ambition did not reach higher than a pair of bell spurs, Mexican hat, pitching pony, and a lariat. In conversation I did not use much of their *rancho* idiom; and my language, though in plain English and of grammatical structure, was a speech so tangled and misunderstood by them that it often elicited a look from them that struck the veritable "greenness" in me of which I was so unmercifully accused. In those days if any one, soberly raised at home and inexperienced, could withstand the batteries of humor in the West with unblenched look, he was certainly a marvel to the people there. They would call him "green from the States," and if he was not satisfied they would prove it to him. They would have him holding a sack for snipes, roasting the bone of a wild turkey's leg for the dainty marrow it contains, believing the distant crowing of prairie chickens to be the cry of mourners for their dead, or in some way or by some strategy have him going through the most dreaded ordeal of a green, inexperienced boy from the States —mounted on and exercised by a flank-girded pitching pony that never knows when to stop till the girt breaks, which you may rely on never happens if they have the fixing of it.

Nothing can compensate for the inexperience of a young man seeking his fortune in the West. He should know how much confidence to place in his fellow-kind—some place too much, some not enough. The error of losing confidence in all, because of the treachery of a few, is a bad philosophy to adopt in life's course. I know nothing more unbecoming, that sets a man more off to himself, than to be soured with everybody. There are good, honest people in the world, and they are to be found everywhere.

Launched out and inexperienced as I was, it was my fault to believe too much that fell from the lips of every one. The people all appeared honest to me in the country I left. I regarded them only as types of mankind generally. There were men whom I should have believed in all things. They were my friends, as they were of every stranger-boy whom they met. There were others who were outwardly equally as clever, as kind as any; but there was a background in their nature, ugly and dark, hidden from the view of my inexperienced eye.

How to believe, how to estimate, how to solve the problem among these, has often been the task of the inexperienced stranger-boy. He is certain to find conclusions, but in these he is often wrong. In this event he is always sure to "pay dear for his whistle." It is then only a matter of time as to when he will be fleeced, for fleecing is verily the profession of some men. The wool falls from only a few sheep before shearing-time.

I would repeat that a boy setting out to find his fortune among strangers needs proper experience and education above every other commodity. I believe, however, that scholars are all apt in this and rapidly advance. No lesson need be repeated, yet a young man may be financially ruined by a single stroke. His eyes in that event are sure to expand, the pupils will take in more light. In all his future action he sees better what he is doing. He knows more of man. His mind now being given more to meditation, he acquires more solidity of step. If never before, he begins now to put away childish life.

My First Speculation—Land Certificates—Fraud.

There seems to be a negative end to every thing. All society has its cheats. All new countries have their sharpers. There is a class of men to be found almost everywhere whose trade is to live by swindling—a kind of remorseless, soulless class of beings, without moral inclination, and the negative ends of all that is worthy and virtuous in society. The field open for these in the earlier days in Texas was to run a trade in land certificates. The government of Texas issued these and sold them. They were genuine; but perhaps nothing was ever more easily counterfeited.

I resolved to find my fortune by becoming the proprietor of Texas lands. I located as much land as I was able to buy certificates for—engaged in business, made more money, and located more lands. Just as I thought my foundation was broad and good, a leaf turned in my history, and I saw plainly that my land speculations were a sad failure. Every certificate was conceived in fraud and "brought forth in iniquity." All that little sum of three or four hundred dollars I carried with me to Texas, together with nearly a year's earnings, in one reversing whirl "went under." It appears like a small affair now, but it was a large one to me then.

I found myself on the broad plain from which all beginnings start. I felt for a little while that the battering-rams of men and nature were against me. I thought of home, sweet home, and the loved ones there. I felt in no mood to return there, though the storm-wind of life was pelting me sore, and full in front. I resolved to breast the storm and yet ride on the tide. This is the thought that laid in me the foundation for a successful life, though I knew it not. I had yet remaining in me all the innocency of heart which I had when I left home, sweet home. What is money, thought I, lands, in comparison with conscious innocence? I had been swindled, it is true, yet I had wronged no one. I had lost money, which is a perishable thing, but I had preserved my integrity.

Turned Pedagogue—Whisky.

Necessity is called the mother of invention. Of course my necessity pressed me into something, and there was no time to be lost. I had now been in the school of experience for a year, had graduated into a much better knowledge of the true character of my fellow-man, but, in order to gain this accomplishment, likewise into poverty. In casting around for business I resolved to turn teacher, and see, while I improved my finances, what I could do for the intellectual and moral improvement of Texas. I soon found myself pleasantly enough engaged, considering the times, in a new, growing, and beautiful town not many miles from Red River.

Teaching school in Texas in those days required much force of will on the part of the teacher. I occupied the court-house, which was in the middle of the square, and which was a building of only one room—a wood building, unceiled, weather-boarded with common clapboards, and wood shutters hung on hinges for windows; a house ungainly and uncomfortable enough, yet the only one in the young city unoccupied. It was "beautiful of situation," in the center of the square, the joy of the whole town. Every day in the week there was much noise on every side of the square in the way of driving, whooping, and swearing, but much more on some days than on others. The great body of the people were clever and civil, but the few rude ones, because the laws in those days were not strictly enforced, presented things in the aspect of general uncivilization.

In those days whisky was sold by the quart as its least legal dimension, unless by special license. Many a man in Texas then did not feel, as the shades of the evening gathered round, that he had shouldered the responsibilities of the day as a pioneer should unless between suns he—to use his own phraseology—had "belted a legal measure." They had a sort of law or custom in their ring that every man must treat. The result was every man of their ring at night-fall carried a quart—at least, as many of them as were able to carry themselves.

It was always a sad picture to me, to see the townsmen in the shades of approaching night gathering up the *débris* of men slain under the pressure of a "legal measure." On many an evening I have looked out of the windows of my court-house school-room and have seen half a dozen or more of these men, even careless of heat of sun on a summer's day, sitting on old goods-boxes or other relics, looking down on the "legal quart" of hell placed in the center of their ring; and now again lifting it to their lips and quaffing down the venomous liquid that drives morality and every ennobling virtue from the heart. Again, such hellish words as escaped their lips! It was enough to chill the blood and astound the senses of every sober-minded youth. I am glad, dear mother, for the pains you took with me, and for the impressive moral lessons you gave me in the formative state of my mind and heart. For these, which have always guarded me in evil hour, I pray you accept my deep-felt gratitude and thanks.

THE ACQUAINTANCE AND HISTORY OF TWO YOUNG DOCTORS.

Here I made the acquaintance of two young men from Tennessee. Noble men they were, of good culture, and of course of good families. They were doctors by profession. Our hearts seemed to be tuned in unison. Never in the West did I feel happier in acquaintanceship. Often, when I had finished my daily task in the school-room, we three naturally met as brother loves brother, and took an evening stroll down a beautiful plateau southward from town. On these occasions we deplored the ruin of many a young man in the West. None of us thought then that we would ever tipple. No, we each felt too much innocency of heart; we remembered too well the moral lessons of our youth; we had too much love for those we left behind; we had too much respect for our own manhood.

But alas poor feeble man! how little he knows of his nature! how little he realizes the life before him! Shall I tell it to you? Yes, I know you want to hear it. I will turn this leaf to view, though it pains my heart to look on the sad picture.

One evening young Elliott accompanied me alone down the plateau, our favorite walking-ground. He appeared unusually reticent. At last, half mournfully, he said, "Do you know where Scott is?" I answered, "No." "Well," said he, "I am afraid they have won him away from us. I would never have thought it, but he is under the influence of alcohol now." "What! Scott?" said I; "Scott, who was our genial companion, and who has been with us so often in our walks on this beautiful plateau?" Elliott was silent, and seemed deeply merged in his own meditations.

Scott was never with us any more. Elliott and I for awhile kept up our evening walks on that beautiful plateau of ground, but when we found Scott with us no more they lost their interest, and gradually ceased altogether.

But here is the sequel of the whole story. Elliott, who told of Scott's first moral delinquency, and was so deeply affected over it, died from the effects of ardent spirits while in the State Legislature. What has become of Scott I know not. So long as I kept his history he was growing worse, more and more departed from what he might have been. Such is human frailty; such is life here below. I often think what a risk I have run in the West. How narrow have been my chances! There is a great deal in training children. The young men of whom I have spoken doubtless were almost properly trained, yet their youthful lessons lacked a little of impressiveness. Methinks, dear mother, if you had trained those noble young men when boys they would not have yielded to temptation.

How Innocency is Taken out of the Human Heart.

I have seen enough history, and have made observations enough, to know how innocency is expelled from the human heart. She sits a modest guard in early life. While we acknowledge the moral decrepitude of human nature entailed from original transgression, yet we claim the latent virtues of the human soul may always be brought to the surface by early and proper training. There need be no exceptions. It is emphatically a possibility. Training children is the worst managed affair that ever entered my meditations. Training properly is the exception to the rule. As long as this matter is so lightly regarded we will have our long court terms, long lists of crimes, reeling drunkards, and well-filled prisons. O that parents would feel the weight of responsibility that rests on them in training their children! A Christian mother in molding the character of her loved boy is engaged in woman's noblest work.

If proper environments are around the youthful mind and heart in any half-way sense in early life, innocency shudders and her nature revolts when any companion enters whose presence pollutes the air she breathes—he is not a congenial spirit; but if a stranger enters with a degree of modesty like herself, yet hiding from the view some mean trait of character, she blushes not in disgust. He is entertained; a genial friendship springs up, and she divides her realm of heart with him. Another stealthily wins his way to the human heart, and takes a seat beside innocency on her throne. Again another and another, until the human heart is parceled out, and instead of an innocent governess ruling supreme, the kingdom is spoiled by partition, and the vices of the age that tend to ruin exert dominant sway. There can be, as a rule, no sudden transition from virtue to sin, from innocence to crime. The work is gradual.

A Scene on the Square Around my Court-house School-room.

Well do I remember a day when intense excitement pervaded every side of the square in the center of which I taught my little school. It was from early morning like a rising cloud of hate, revenge, and bitterness, and it grew more lowering as the hours rolled by. It seemed that all enemies had met for once, and all feuds contested; that the furies of nature had assembled at one place to do their best. Whisky was ruling supreme. Ere the sun had reached his zenith, the very air appeared polluted with horrid oaths. As the day passed on, the loud talking gradually lulled into a repeated thud-like growl. That indicated the time was fully up, and that whatever business was to be done must be immediately dispatched.

It was one of those occasions in which you need not look to see—in which you need not be told; you comprehended the situation by drinking in the air around. Who that has proper convictions of rectitude and virtue could feel indifference for this frenzied hour? What boy could sit still in the court-room school-house when he could look through the windows and see the *mêlée* in which his father was engaged. I pulled to the plank shutters. It made the room dark—too dark for study. I wanted to close my eyes and the eyes of those intrusted to my care against the dark, revolting picture displayed around. More than once an urchin sprung to his feet, and begged to be let out, that he might see how his father fared.

By and by the storm of day abated. Meditative steps are heard and modulated tones of voice. Many have left the town who were foremost in the fray. I open the windows and let in the light of day. Comparative quiet reigns without. We resume our school-room duties, not knowing the casualties of the day. ·Believe me when I say the picture is not overdrawn. Believe me again when I say a large majority of Texas citizens did not participate in such degrading actions, nor sympathize with a course so degrading and so lost to true manhood. The reckless spirit and lawlessness of a few gave the appearance among the many.

Only one instance will I cite as illustrative of the day. In the shades of the evening my attention was called by the moans I heard in a little hotel. Stepping into it, lying on a couch I saw a most pitiable object — the same young doctors of whom I have already spoken busily engaged in taking up broken arteries and trying, if possible, to check the flow of blood. This was in the days of their innocency. The object on whom they were operating to my astonishment was club-footed. I learned afterward that through the heat of whisky he was as fierce as any. Hence the sad picture he presented at close of day.

About Dancing.

On one occasion while in pleasant mood I was passing to my boarding-house I heard on my left a romping sound. I stopped, looked, and saw the whirl of human beings. Now moving around altogether with thundering sound; now again all still, with faces front, while one with limping step now to the right, and now to the left again, with corresponding gyrations queer and odd, until, like an acting magnet, one of the other sex, who now refreshed by rest, with toe more light and gyrations more humorous, starts to meet the figure form before him. Now they approach each other; now they recede again; now as puppets moved by wires they pass each other, he to the right and she to the left; now they turn and try it the other way, with skipping and hopping and physical contortions funny and queer. Having shown each other all the bodily gyrations and steps of the toe they had learned, with tired limb and panting breath they for support seize each other by the hands, and round and round in dizzy whirl they finish. Then, with a consciousness of having done their best, looking love in each other's eyes, they retire to the line of the circle formed side by side. No sooner done than another figure form is out with toe as light, and another, until each one has had a chance and each one has done his best. Then again, hand in hand, round and round with thundering sound they all move together.

What pedagogue would not stop after his day's labor and mental strain are finished and see such humorous sport? What traveler either among the Orientals or in the Western World would not deem it good luck to happen on such a scene? Why, surely this is a felicitous occasion for the pen of the traveler or the pencil of the artist. I will inquire something of this, thought I; and so after looking awhile at the funny, humorous action of the company assembled there, thinking that I had no more time to spare, I soon reached the door-sill of my boarding-house. The old pioneer with whom I boarded was in.

"Colonel," said I, "I am a little behind time, but you just ought to go up yonder where that noise is and see something that beats P. T. Barnum or any clown East or West."

"Why," said the Colonel, "do n't you know that a dancing-master has arrived in town, and some of the silly people are going crazy after him? He is showing the people now how to appear in society. He is going to teach the people the use of their toes and manners. He has made a school to-day of forty scholars, and will begin his course of instruction to-morrow."

I believe the Colonel was going to say more, but a couple of gentlemen stepping in broke as an interlude into his speech. He might have said many good things on the subject and the morals of the people, for he had gifts and grace, and but little patience with the intrusion of a dancing-master or any thing of like type which oxygenates public morals. The gentlemen were members of a committee, under instruction to see me and if possible get me to suspend my school and give the dancing-master a chance; that the time he required was short, only two weeks; that many of my pupils would attend his school in order to learn the use of the "toe and manners."

"Gentlemen," said I, "it is not for the sake of two weeks that I assume my position—it is not for any pecuniary advantage they can possibly afford me that I assume my position; it is on the broad ground of morality and virtue. Your request is most wretchedly unreasonable, and should I entertain it, I would be guilty of classing myself second to a dancing-master, which I shall never do, though the stars fall. I am young, it is true, though I think I have a mature judgment in this case. If your dancing-master educates the heel, I wish you to understand that I am educating the mind and heart. Judge you who will implant solid manners, but be sure and "judge righteous judgment." As the teacher of your school, I claim the right to assess the guilt of my students, and to punish accordingly. If I am unreasonable, and incur guilt on myself, your recourse is to the statutes of the State. I here announce to you that any student of mine who shall attend the dancing-school shall be expelled, and that this shall in no wise exempt the parents of such from payment of tuition."

The foregoing is as nearly as I can remember the speech I made to those gentlemen of the committee appointed to wait on me. It had an awakening influence on the citizens. My school went regularly on. The dancing-school was likewise taught through. By it much of the people's money was taken away, morality made worse, and consequently the manners of the people unimproved. At the close of the dancing-school two delinquent students of mine returned. I sent them back home as expelled. The parents came and protested against my action. I showed them my law. They apologized and promised. The conditions justified me in kindly receiving their children again. I have never, to this day, heard of a dancing-master in that town again. The whole affair shows a characteristic of the people of a new country. They are a little too much inclined to fall into line with what is popularly going, without considering its *ultimatum*.

A Plan to Regain my Lost Fortune.

It was while I was still engaged here that I conceived the plan of regaining my loss in the certificate swindle which I had sustained. The Colonel with whom I boarded was surveyor of a land district that embraced several counties in area. He was a candidate for reëlection, and told me that in the event he was successful in the race he would give me a deputyship in the business. He said that he needed an active young man in the field; that he was getting old, and would do the office-work. This was pleasing news to me, and as I by education understood the theory of surveying and had some practice in the field, I felt ready at any time to take up chain and compass. There were hundreds of thousands of acres of land to locate in the district, and I could get all the work I could do in locating lands on the shares for men who had genuine certificates.

I must say just at this juncture that school-teaching now appeared to me to be a little business—entirely too small for one who felt the prospect and capacity for surveying which I did, and who looked in fond anticipation to many fold more profit. I felt assured that the Colonel would be elected. He was an honest pioneer, a Christian gentleman—not a craving man, having great opportunities for wealth yet not amassing much of this world's goods. He had a prestige for frontier activity and Indian-fighting that merited respect and confidence. He was in the memorable encounter in which the lamented Colonel Denton was killed. I thought this man honest, and I have never changed my opinion of him to this day.

The office being in those days a very lucrative one made it very desirable. This officer, though poor on the day of his election, might during the term of his office, by industry, become possessed of a large land estate. The Colonel, or present surveyor, always had a good character up to this time; but the friends of his opponent, as I thought and still think, in a most dastardly manner turned a leaf in his history, which if true would blacken the character of a man sufficiently to render him more fit for the companionship of demons than of men. It may be the interest I took in the election rendered me an improper judge in the case. However this may be, it was the opinion I had of the man before the contest, and it was general then; and I heard nothing of it after the election.

On the day of election every advantage, honorable and disreputable, was taken. Intrigue, fraud, and lying banded themselves together in their most becoming aspect. Voters were bought when the conscience of the man would not revolt. The merit of a favored candidate was lauded to the skies. Dubious things became positive truths or positive lies, just to suit the cause. Opinions were emphasized with ungodly epithets, and passion rose on the smallest contradictions. Whisky was drunk by quarts without the money of those who gurgled it down. But the day passed by, the votes were counted. The Colonel was beaten by a majority of two votes. As a matter of course, my prospective financial policy was ended. No line was now open to me but, with an easy conscience, to continue my little school.

How I Made Atonement for Being a Partisan.

Old Tray is represented as a good-natured spaniel. Unluckily he was caught in bad company, and had to suffer. I do not to this day think I was in bad company. I was simply allied with the Colonel's party. This was my crime, though I felt not the pang of it nor felt its stain. It looked unphilosophical to me, yet the young school-teacher, for the crime of being an honest partisan, had to suffer, all for party prejudice—that tyrant which when unbridled rides down innocency with a harlequin look; that knows no mercy, respects no claim, but looks solely to party aggrandizement; that foolish imp that frames all its reasonings for a certain end, not considering whether it be right or wrong; that hound of the infernal depths that laughs at the misery of one-half of mankind, delights in pulling society to pieces, and gives a lamentable howl when both truth and virtue prevail.

Another school was soon established in another quarter of the little town, and now like two hives of bees—no, let us not in the comparison degrade the useful honey-making articulates that can sting but once and then die, but like two nests of wasps whose proximity has brought fierce combat between the members, each of which can sting a hundred times a day and then rest better through the night. Many a time a day it pierces, wounds, and poisons; and every time one is pierced it raises his anger more. From early morn till late at eve the combat grows; nor even does a Sabbath intervene to give the parties rest, till at last, weary of mind or tired of monotonous toil, their angers droop and they turn to things more novel. Thus it is when party spirit rules the heart and frenzies the brain of man. In this kind of heat, if a deed is to be done, howsoever dark it may be, whether by the tongue or hand lifted high, there lives the man, if he is only sought, that will perform the act. In order to perform the most villianous deeds, search only need be made till the man is found.

Disgust—Musings—Looking to the Legal Profession.

I grew weary at the beholding. I love society, and nothing can win me away from congenial spirits. But when people forget their high origin and smelt their natures into the putridness of hate, jealousy, backbiting, and envy—of lying for party preference, without counting the cost to society, without realizing the worth of man, moral and intellectual—then to me that quarter of the earth is a stench to my nostrils; it presents to my mind a loathsomeness of aspect, and has a plague in its atmosphere, against which my nature revolts.

I resolved at the close of my school to find a place where there was union and peace—where society had no mildew upon it. I wanted to find a place where the granite rocks of love and friendship cropped out in pyramidal piles; where charity flowed as a peaceful river; where the sun rose in love, shone in beauty, and set in splendor. I left the storm behind, and retired to a country-seat. It was a delightful change.

Here was aroused in me anew the feeling I had experienced in my boyhood days. It was the promptings of an ambition that for sometime had been latent. Political life in early boyhood had for me a charm that made me feel restless. I loved its public discussions. The excitement came over me afresh while in my retirement. I appeared to myself like one just waking up to proper reflections on his proper course of life. Dreams of promotion would sometimes pass before my vision. However, I was yet on the plain from which all beginnings start. Who is a benefactor to me? thought I. I am only a young man in the West, tossed up and down, full of mistakes and changing events; now looking for some sheltering rock where rest may be found.

Yes, thought I, though a stranger, there is a chance for me, and I will abide my time with patience. Moral worth is a good introduction, the very best commodity for a young rising man. It is this that will in time give him prestige. Let him only keep this, and combine with it intellectual culture and industry, and the indications of his mind will be conceived by the advocates of right principles. As a step before the public, I resolved on the study of the law. This I did not do, perhaps, as the student ordinarily enters on this profession—for the living that is in it. I had an ambition that reached beyond the mere practice of the profession. My object was to use the profession of the law as a means of attaining unto the *ultimatum* of my ambition. However much I might have needed the living to be found in the practice of the law, yet it did not enter my thoughts only in some secondary sense. The resolutions of my mind were the following: I will study the law; I will do my best to know it thoroughly; when I enter on the profession, I will never take a case which I shall know to be wrong; I will ever be ready to help the innocent; I will discipline myself to the most rigid moral rectitude.

In this view I procured books and entered on a course of reading. I became more fond of books than ever before in my life. I seemed to myself to be in a hurry; I found myself continually hurrying up; I was anxious to be before the people. In my spirit, which perhaps was a little too sanguine, I calculated on success. This thought, continually recurring, kept me comfortable. When I talked, I talked of the law and what I had been reading; when I walked, I meditated and digested. I loved to look into the problem of right and wrong, to run hair-lines of distinction, and see the very beginnings of turpitude and crime.

If ever a man was overwhelmingly engaged in a study, I seemed to be that one; if ever a man was decided on a course of life, it was I. Yet, shades of the night! if you ask me if I ever practiced or had a client, I will say no; if you ask me if I ever picked up the gauntlet of a political opponent, I will say no; if you ask me if I ever finished the study of the law, I answer no; if you ask me if my life has been a happy one notwithstanding, I say yes.

FINDING AT LAST MY PROPER LIFE BUSINESS.

At this period in my history a greater change came over me than at any period of my life. In this period *life's business became fully confirmed unto me.* True, I had resolved on political life as most congenial to my nature. I was now arduously engaged in the study of the law as a stepping-stone to that business. This I preferred to every other. Nothing seemed to move before my imagination like unto the principles of true government, the philosophy of the minds of the governed, legislative assemblies and their proceedings. This idea seemed planted in me, like a principle born in my nature. To pluck it up by the roots required the strength of an omnipotent hand. To change my life from its intentions and fancies, after I had resolved to run it on principles as solid as the rocks and as pure as gold, was not a mortal act. I had no fear of moral decline in the business of my selection. The base on which I resolved to stand I knew would support me. I had seen in my short career in the West many a man fall from my side—some whom I loved most dearly, and whom I hated to give up; yet I felt daily that I was more strongly intrenched in the paths of virtue and honor. Every one who had fallen from my side was a lesson to me never to be forgotten. Happiness seemed just ahead, and all I had to do, thought I, was to steer on, and my now small and scarcely navigable river would open into a deep, wide, and smooth sea.

But, shades of the night! I found myself steering my life in a kind of human speculative sense, basing all my success on human ingenuity and power—giving my consent, however, fully to all the truths of the Christian religion. My life, however, in order to render it less liable to err, needed more grace—more of that principle that branches deepest in virtue, and gives an assurance that it will end in eternal fruition. I became very meditative, and would unconsciously hold up my own heart to view. It did not have the innocent appearance it had to me when I was a boy by your side and from day to day heard your kindly words. The West had not left me altogether unscathed; yet I had done no overt act against either the human or divine law that smote my conscience. The point that hurt me most was general neglect of duties. I resolved to make amends, repented, and felt better.

I went to my books, but I found myself in unrest and unattempered to use them as once I did. Like a trace continually breaking, I yet hitched on again, until in disgust I left the business for a walk into a grave-yard. Here I stopped to ponder over life and all mortal things. Here I sat, I stood, I walked, I meditated, I prayed. I felt the throes of a revolution going on in my moral nature.

Many things came up in my memory that had long lain forgotten. When a little boy I had joined the Church. In those days I had many a struggle, and hardly contested many a field in my own simple innocent way. Some of my acts then appear to me now quite silly and foolish; yet many others appear full wise enough for their day. I remembered well that when a boy I promised most sincerely that I would be a preacher when proper years of discretion should come, and I remembered that I had repeated this promise time and again; but the most forcible remembrance, and that which made me shudder most, was the truant part I had played.

Why did I go to the West? thought I. Simply to seek my fortune there? No, that was not all. That standing alone suppresses part of the truth. Verging into manhood as I was, I felt a growing independency of spirit. My individuality began to assert its claims. A cold indifference came over me for religion and all moral good. O what a crisis a young man has to pass through! There is a time when he needs help, patience, the kindliest admonitions. There is a period in the history of every young man's life in which he is sorely tried. I would place it from seventeen to twenty-one years of age. Changes are continually going on in him during this period. You see it in the changes of his voice, in his manners, in his plans, in the general bent of his nature, to assert his own individuality. This is the age that gives the most trouble to teachers and the greatest uneasiness to parents. It is the most formative period of our existence, for it is the period in which judgment begins to play a part, and consequently of rejecting and accepting. What is true of boys and young men applies with equal aptness to the other sex, only this formative period is of younger years.

I remembered my promise. I knew I ought to fill it; but no, the responsibility was too great—this is not the business of my liking. Here was the darkest day of my history, a day in which no light broke on my moral vision; no friendly voice cheered my heart; no rainbow of promise spanned my moral sky. I sunk myself away in the seclusion of solitude, and locked my heart away from all human thought, and carefully kept the problem all to myself. Now, "to him that is afflicted pity should be shown." But I got no pity, because I did not make known my affliction. Here I resolved that I would be a preacher after the lapse of two years. On the promise my conscience became somewhat easy. In the meantime I resolved to go West and leave, for awhile at least, these lands where my independence and individuality were restrained.

Now, dear mother, if I had confessed to you the state of my mind and heart, I would have found the comfort needed. How readily would you through word and token have helped me out of the slough into which I had fallen! and I, at an earlier day, might have been in the ministry at your door, and not after a lapse of time, so far away. But I, in my foolishness, resolved to fight my battles in an independent way, not appreciating a mother's helping hand. It was a strange forgetfulness in me.

I had been in Texas for more than the stipulated time with which I eased my conscience. During that time, twice I had placed my stakes for a fortune, but just as often realized the vanity of all things here below. I had fully discovered that a man may chase a bubble in fond anticipations, but that it may burst in a moment most unexpected, and with it vanish all fond hopes. Shall I give up the law with all my outgrowing anticipations? thought I. Yes, I resolved to give it up and let it go to the winds. This may prove but another bursting bubble, and I will pursue it no farther; it is but another cheat of man's own making; it is but one of those delusive fancies that may never bring happiness: I will discard it at once and add it to the list of vanities; I will no longer trifle with an omnipotent hand that has always kindly led me and been long-suffering toward me. I gave up my own will, bowed my head, and He took me. God wanted me as one of his special agents. O wonderful, wonderful!

Now I remember, dear mother, just at this time I wrote you a long letter. I have your reply to it. I have always kept it as one of those cherished mementos too dear and fragrant ever to be lost or forgotten. Brother Fielding will please read for us again:

OUR LETTERS ON THE MINISTRY.

My Dear Mother: This letter will bear you tidings which, perhaps, will awaken in you a little surprise. There has been a great revolution in my moral nature and feeling. I am impressed to-day that I am established on a rock whose base is sure and steadfast. I am called to the ministry of the gospel of Christ. I have accepted the situation with a feeling of unworthiness, and yet of astonishment and wonder. There is no doubt in my mind that it is the will of God that I should bear a part of life's burdens in the capacity of a preacher. The great wonder to me is that one so unworthy should be raised to an office so high. I think now that I shall find a higher enjoyment in this than in any other course of my life, although I have by no means attained unto it by choice. My ambition ran in another channel in which there is less sacrifice and much worldly honor. I have had a hard contest to quit the line of former intentions; yet I have at last yielded, and find pleasure in yielding.

I now forcibly realize the fact that every man has a mission here below, and that is that the world should be made better by his existence; but the trouble is, many do not accept the situation. The world is too cold and selfish, and the individuals who compose it have too little concern beyond self. This ought to be a peaceful, happy world; and it can only be made so through the mission of Christ. As an agent in his hand and under his superior guidance, I sincerely desire, in a humble way, to put in my strength to ameliorate the condition of mankind and point them to the ultimate rest.

I do not realize now that I am tossed up and down in the earth for want of employment. There can now be no longer intermission in my life business. Every man is my neighbor and God is my friend. My nearest alliance is with Christ. The world is the field of my operation; and in this, the same as in every thing I have attempted in life, I shall do my best, by the grace of God. The life before me is one of arduous toil and sacrifice, I know. The highest reward attainable here is the enjoyment which springs from a full consciousness of an entire submission to the will of God and consecration to the work; but in the end will come the full fruition. Who can contemplate the indescribable happiness of the man who through a life-time has borne the cross of Christ with undeviating rectitude, and feels that all is peace as he looks toward his going-down sun? Who can tell the joy of him, in such a time, who through life has not sought personal preferment, but who through sacrifice has looked to the interest of his fellow-kind?

The line in which I have been given a place has a grand history. If I should want to find the most beautiful specimens of moral heroism of which the earth can boast, I would only follow this line back through the centuries to Christ. The list is headed by Paul, the grandest hero of ancient or modern times; and all along is a heroism in sacrifice that would never have enriched the earth only through faith in the promises. It is a noble history. The society is the finest of earth, the company the noblest. I feel that I am in the enjoyment of a wonderfully grand promotion.

I know I have had your help all along—your admonitions before

I left, and your prayers since every day. True merit shall not go unrewarded, though we are all "unprofitable servants." I need not ask you to pray on, and especially for my steadfastness; I know this you will do. I trust this exaltation given me may prove a blessing to you; and if you ever feel oppressed by gloom, and the shades of night gather around your moral sky, remember God has hunted down your son and made him a preacher in the West. Cheer up, mother; cheer up, and look toward your eastern sky. It looks a long way off; yet all the way down your life has flowed as a peaceful river. Now look toward your western sky; see, it is getting nearer as the rolling years glide by. Does it not look beautiful? Your sun is now going down, and mine is going toward his zenith. I know yours will set after awhile with glow and radiance, yet there will be left behind an undying twilight to cheer your preacher-boy, until the waves of this present life are past and he with thee at last has found unceasing rest.

Your son, with true filial devotion,

MOTHER'S REPLY.

My Dear Son: I am not in the least surprised with the tidings of your late letter. My children are all in the hands of God, who has promised to be a father to the orphans. When you were young and only of a few summers, you remember how God thought it best to call my husband from these mortal shores. I then claimed the promise he made, and committed the responsibility of a father to his care, trusting him to supply all needed things. I have shown more wisdom by humble trust in him than in any other course of my life. In every thing else my life has been marred with mistakes and awkwardness, but in this every thing has been in order and brought good results. Faith is the foundation of all true wisdom. No, I am not surprised at all. God knows best what to do with his children. In answering your letter, I feel my own unworthiness, and yet a deep-felt gratitude to God for such a favor as he has bestowed on me—calling one of my sons to the high office of the ministry. This more than repays me for all my toils, diligence, and faith. While I cannot say it is the reward of my own virtue, yet I know virtue never goes unrewarded. It is enough for me to know that Heaven is working the highest respectability in my own family by calling one of my children and conferring on him so high an office.

God, by whom all things are made, is continually superintending his moral universe as well as governing the physical. The grandest display of his moral influence we find in the atonement made for sin by Jesus Christ. All other demonstrations look small in the comparison. Yet choosing as he does to work through agencies, he does a little here and a little there. When it is all summed up and we look at the whole, we are struck with awe at the vastness of the work he is doing through agencies; yet *he* is in it all. God as certainly calls men to office in his moral government now as in any preceding age of the world's history. He has begun a work and, has not left it to the whims and caprice of men, but in time, by the sway of his power, through his government in direct operation and through his agents, will yet prove to the whole world the true merit and worth to man of Mary's Son. He has, seemingly in mercy to me, but more through the wisdom of his own choice, taken you into the army of his public servants. Son, this is a high enrollment; be true to your colors.

Your life, I trust, will be one of much happiness; yet you will have many things to endure for Christ's sake. The eyes of the world will now be upon you more than ever before; your correctest manner will be criticised by many. The least derelictions on your part will be magnified into great sins; you will learn much by looking deep down into your own nature and heart; and whatever you find wrong there, by correcting it, you will have to be more deliberate, and meditate more than you speak. Do nothing and say nothing without a consciousness that it is right. Above all, live near to *Him* whose cause you have espoused, and who has taken you into the high office of the ministry.

I have observed that it is not every one who is called that does good. It is only they who magnify that calling. Nothing, in my estimation, presents so sad and lamentable a picture as the manner of a minister of the gospel not corresponding with his high office. Light and chaffy conversation are alike degrading in the minister of Christ. He should be sober-minded, his topics well chosen, and all his words of decent English.

The minister of the gospel should be ambitious; not, however, in the ordinary sense of that word—seeking personal aggrandizement; but in a holy, consecrated sense—striving after a high attainment in science, literature, and theology. In this way he will have a more congenial way of reaching the different classes of men. No other than a cultivated man, full up with the age in which he lived, could have with impunity preached Christ unto the Athenians from Mars'

Hill. Yet Paul did this, and successfully introduced Christ. While Paul stood a success at Mars' Hill, a thousand carelessly living behind their age of the world would have fallen in the effort. Paul was so scholarly, and so well up with the age in which he lived, that he needed less of the *upper* guardianship than some men. The grandest display of Heaven in his case was to break his Judaistic neck and inure him to the yoke of Christ. I hope you perceive this hint. God will never do for a man what man can do for himself. He will only supply man with the things he needs and of which he is incapable. Some, in a mistaken way, look for more than necessary help from God. In this way life passes, and but little is known and done. The minister of the gospel must be studious.

I shall entertain no doubt but that you will succeed in your new and high calling, and that you will be a humble instrument in doing much good. I know something of your manners and diligence. I am glad you have yielded, and have fought no longer against the claims high Heaven has on you. It would have been a sad day in my history to learn that you stubbornly opposed the Spirit of grace through your love for other things. I certainly, in that event, could have found no pleasure in following the history of a son so recreant to the Spirit's high calling.

I am not surprised that you have turned preacher, by the grace of God. Well do I remember that when twelve years of age you resolved on reading the Bible through, and carried out the resolution that same year. Many happy hours did I spend in those days as I beheld you digging in the rich mines of God's sacred word. Even then I indulged the hope that God would find some special use for you. I could not find the true state of your heart then, on account of your reticence on personal experience. Go on, then, in faith and diligence, my son, and you will finally obtain your reward.

Your affectionate mother,

REFLECTIONS ON A CALL TO THE MINISTRY.

Now, dear mother, there are some who do not look at a call to the ministry as I do. There is a kind of speculative idea in the world that all men are under obligations to God, and that they are free to preach or otherwise, just as it may suit their conscience, or as the Church may appoint. I think it is well enough for the Church to exercise an oversight in the matter, but by no means repudiate the fact that God this day and through all time will call men through his word and through the direct operation of his Spirit to fill certain missions in this life, and more especially the ministry of his word. All the talk in the world and arguments of men could not change my mind that it is my bounden duty to preach the gospel, and that it is made plainly so on my mind and heart through the influence of God and his word.

TROUBLES AND EMBARRASSMENTS OF STARTING.

After I was licensed to preach, I felt a strange gloominess creep over me. I constantly desired and sought solitude. My happiness came more by my own meditations than through converse with my fellow-kind. I was content with what I had done and with my new relation to society, yet the highest pressure of unrest was upon me. Full of anxiety in this new sphere of activity, burning with ardor to find how to begin, a revolution of impatience pervaded all the precincts of my mind and nature. I felt a desire to go out among strangers as a more congenial way of beginning. But where shall I go and exhibit myself in this new relation, drawn by the Spirit, and yet as if by haste and magic? I was like the man who commenced building his house without first sitting down and counting the cost. Ah! how always since I pity the young candidate for the ministry! Poor fellow! he must obey the call of the Master, yet how soon he feels the burdens of the cross! How soon he realizes that entering the ministry is like entering no other business! I do always from the depth of my heart sympathize with the young man as I see him entering the ministry.

In the midst of my embarrassments, I concluded to go to the vicinity of my old ranch, about twenty miles west of where I was licensed to preach, and make my first efforts there. I knew many of the people in this vicinity. As I came near the neighborhood, I wondered how I should make known the fact that I was a licensed preacher. This was a very annoying thought to me, for I felt conscious they had never heard of the change wrought in me. I was relieved of this embarrassment, however, unexpectedly and handsomely enough. There was a good-meaning, clever citizen, a member of the Baptist Church, living on my ranch. His quick eye, notwithstanding my efforts to look as usual, discovered that a perceptible change had come over me. After the usual compliments, he said with an anxious look, "What is the matter with you?"

"Nothing unusual, I suppose," said I.

"Yes, but," said he, "I know there is something. There has come some kind of a change over you."

This was all very strange to me, indeed quite problematical. I have since attributed it to the unusual seriousness that had permeated my whole being now for nearly a month. In reply, said I: "My friend, I suppose I shall have to give you a little speck of my history, which will probably explain all you desire to know. I am now, sir, a licensed preacher; but I did not know till now that it had made a change in my appearance. I have recently been licensed to preach by a Quarterly Conference of the Methodist Episcopal Church, South. This is a high office, and I feel a great degree of unworthiness for such a relation as I now sustain. Your surprise at my appearance is no greater than my own at finding myself in this new relation to society."

"Well," said he, "I had much rather you had been a Baptist."

"That," said I, "I can never be, and for reasons I am not now in a mood to give."

"Well," said he, "we must have preaching anyhow. We don't get much of it in this Western country. Methodist preaching is better than none. I suppose you are willing to preach for us."

"Yes," said I, "I am willing to do what I can. I have not made a beginning yet, but I am willing and ready any day to try. But when shall I preach and where, for you know we have no churches in this country?"

"Preach right here in this house," said he, "next Sunday; I will see that you have a congregation."

"Thank you, my friend," said I. Indeed, this was quite a surprise to me, and a very welcome one, for it took away quite a load of embarrassment.

MY FIRST SERMON.

When Sunday came, I was overwhelmed with surprise to find so many people assembling. For miles around they came—from Hickory Creek, Clear Creek, and Denton Creek, and from other places wherever a frontiersman had domiciled himself anywhere in reach. They came, men, women, and children, with their dogs and a few cats, to hear one of their number—a pioneer, now turned preacher—proclaim the tidings of salvation. I have thought since if my friend on the ranch has done all his life's work as well as he spread the appointment of the new preacher, he is not one against whom the people should complain.

But now the ordeal was at hand, the crisis that most tries the young preacher. He is naturally ambitious, and wants to succeed. A consecrated ambition is a holy thing and a desirable quality. By it he is a student, by it he becomes scholarly; though it is hard for him sometimes, after having done his best, to be content to leave the results with God. He desires to be the peer of any one. He has a high self-respect. He wants to feel that God will supply all lack; yet there rises up in him the consciousness that God will never do for him what he can do for himself. On this ground he feels that he has to be a student and prepare for his ministrations. This beginning is a crisis in the life and experience of all young ministers. It may bring joy or sorrow, pleasure or mortification, kill or make alive.

With much diffidence, at the hour appointed I appeared before my congregation. I, as I thought, went through a tolerable exercise; nothing in it particularly to elate or cast down—good enough for a beginning perhaps, and yet mainly attributable to previous hard study of the subject. My mind was now fully impressed that if a man preached he had to do what is usually done in any profession—prepare himself for the business by hard study. Meditation and prayer would of course occupy their proper places.

I gave notice here of my intention to go into the traveling connection and of being a regular itinerating minister; that I could stay with them only a short time. On this announcement I was requested to preach for them again. This I did two or three times. Then I left them for the Quarterly Conference in which I sought a recommendation. I felt a deep sense of my unworthiness for so high a calling, and a great lack of that knowledge which is necessary for the successful minister of Christ. I had heard several persons preach since I had obtained license, and all appeared in advance of me in the knowledge of God's word and power. I still desired and sought seclusion, and often felt mortified on reflecting on my own incapacity to handle the word of God with a master's hand. A consciousness of my weakness made me resolve to know the Scriptures, to be a hard student of the word of God, to labor to improve myself in all respects, that I might find favor before the people and therefore do good for Christ's sake. However, I embraced no idea more fully than that God would help me only in things which I could not do myself. Hence all my prayers went up in this philosophical and scriptural way.

Going to My First Conference.

I was duly recommended by the Quarterly Conference for trial in the traveling ministry. Only a few days passed before all things were ready, and I found myself *en route* for the city in which the Annual Conference was to be held, a distance of more than two hundred miles. My company of preachers going down were all mounted on horseback—were five in number, making six of us altogether. One like myself just starting, another of two years' experience, highly opinionated in himself, and three others, elderly-like, either in or approaching toward the meridian of their days; all seemingly jocular enough, as though they were out for recreation or on a holiday hunt. I did not feel as they did, nor do I think my friend just starting did. My utmost effort could not shut down the rising tide of seriousness which ramified all the secret cells of my nature, and which at times seemed to burst the dikes and dams of my meditations, and fill me with misgivings and alarm about the great business into which I was entering. In view now that it is past, I am not sorry; but I would shudder to know that the experience were to be repeated. Several times I was chided for my reticence; yet to be otherwise was against my nature. Often I thought if those seniors only knew the half that was in my heart, they would not chide, but sympathy and pity would be awakened as for one that is afflicted. Surely, thought I, they have forgotten their troubles of other days. But our lives here are full of annoyances and mistakes. The flower may look beautiful enough to the eye, but be repulsive to the olfactory; the fruit may look red and inviting, yet be bitter to the taste.

I think preachers need recreation as well as peo-
5

ple of other professions. The highest recreation in Texas in those days among the preachers was found in going to Conference, which was generally a long jaunt on horseback. It was performed in groups of three or half a dozen together. The poor hard-worked fellows had their purses better filled now than at any other season of the year, and if ever they had a full new suit all at once, either had it on or carefully stowed away in their saddle-bags for display in the city of the Conference. The manner of their attire was regarded as a sure index of their financial success, or, to say the least, that they had either been among or not among a clever people. But few questions were asked of any one who seemed to have fared well concerning the people whom he served; no one seemed to care to hear him say that a petition was in for his return, for each one thought the place would do, and if he should at the close of Conference be read out to it, he would only be fortunate.

They usually went to Conference in all sorts of moods for conversation. Now strung out two and two together, or carelessly apart, and now again the whole group together. At one time the conversation low and monotonous, again in a louder tone. At one time seriously engaged in conversation on doctrine, or perhaps more seriously on the trials of itinerant life; but again in reminiscence or anecdote at which sometimes would come bursts of laughter that would make the hills and forests give back the echo round. One is gloomy, he is chided into action; another is reticent, he is rallied; another talks too long on one subject, he is fired into and scattered. Their minds were usually as well stocked with anecdote and humorous incidents as each one's treasury department—the saddle-bags—was of manuscript, books, and his best clothes. No enjoyment ran higher than when they could make one of their number the subject of remark, some incident humorous and really enjoyable having eked out from his lips at an unexpected time and in an unexpected way. He was then the hero of the day.

Any new traveler with them soon becomes convinced that Methodist circuit riders have seen much, heard much, and know much. Their magazines of wit, humor, anecdote, and reminiscence seemingly have had closed doors, awaiting the occasion when the brotherhood take liberty with one another which they do with no one else. On these occasions, every one is presumed to be fully able to take care of himself. If he awkwardly falls into a ditch, he scarcely ever gets a helping hand; if he bogs in a mire, he must clean his own clothes. He gets no quarter, he gives none. He rises by his own ingenuity; he falls by his own weakness. "Be a man" is the idea; nor is it without its fruit of cultivating self-reliance. I was a quiet observer of men and times in those days—more so than ever before or since. I saw some things that rasped my nature. My own mood disqualified me for many things really enjoyable. I could see nothing particularly sinful in my company. It was only the bounding of the spirit which for a short time was relieved from heavy cares. It was a holiday recreation, full of enjoyment, especially to the men already inured to a circuit rider's life.

On some of these occasions there was perhaps a little too much rein given to thought and expression, but some one would soon begin to moralize. Seniors should always be exemplars before the rising buds in the ministry. The young preacher is tender, and needs the most careful nursing. He neither needs to see too much nor to hear too much. All the evidences he gets from his seniors should tend to inspire him with a devotional spirit and the great worth of human souls. He is but a bud yet to bloom, and the tints and coloring of the flower he shall make are yet to appear. He is an imitator, and will find a model somewhere; he has nowhere to go outside of the sphere of his acquaintance to find it, and will naturally find his model among the preachers. Some one of these is sure to be an ideal character. Hence it becomes all seniors to be grave, and especially to avoid lightness and chaffy conversation, which are repugnant to the word of God. This would by no means suppress hilarity of spirit when properly attempered by sober-mindedness. It is no check on anecdote, humor, and wit, when not of a low and vulgar order.

AT CONFERENCE—A SKETCH.

Finally our last day's journey was finished, and we found ourselves at Conference. Here they came, from near and far, to report the summing up of a whole year's stewardship, with "How d' ye" here and "How d' ye" there, with greeting smiles and enjoyable looks, in annual social gathering that the brethren love. We received instruction or obtained guides to our respective boarding-houses during the session. On reaching my boarding-house, I found one had preceded me. As I stepped to the door, I saw him, long and lank, looking as though he had more ribs to the side than usually belong. to men, or else a greater space between them. With semi-guttural tone and nasal twang; with knees too high when sitting, and head too low when standing; linking the mien of a mixed mind with a crooked gait; being the embodiment of importance with the soul of a stray dog; there he sat, as I entered, carelessly, unconcerned about circumstances, with high knees, and an almost neckless head resting on his body—the ill omen of any thing the imagination could work up. While I was musing who the stranger was, the polite landlord came in and soon made known to us this man who so much abused nature in his physical development.

He was a new-comer, with his parchments, from one of the sister Churches, knocking at the door of Methodism to find a place to preach the word, and perhaps along with it to show to the people what the forces which had worked in his physical structure could do for one mortal man. He reminded me of the lost link; and I never doubted, in the event he should succeed in getting an appointment, but that people would meet wherever he appointed to preach or otherwise display—for there are people who go for the gospel's sake, and others to a monkey-show; and where the two are united, the best congregations may be found. Thousands go to hear the gospel, but more to see the enormities of Barnum; and lo! a greater than Barnum was here.

"Had n't orter" was one of his pet phrases, for he was from a State far North, and neither talked nor looked like our people. "Yes," said he, "I am from another Church, but I think the Methodis' do some things they had n't orter do." "What things?" said I. "Why," said he, "I think they had n't orter baptize their babies." Said I: "Sir, you 'had orter' staid where you were, and 'had n't orter' come away. What are you going to do about it if the Conference gives you a circuit?" Said he, "I reckon I had n't orter say any thing about it." This is only a specimen of our conversation. I had no voice on the Conference-floor. I certainly would have stopped this impostor. I privately spoke to some of the brethren of him, but heard nothing of it afterward. I perhaps had gotten more into the inner character of this man than any other.

As this odd character is before me, I will finish with him, and then go back and take up the thread of my narrative. Yes, he got an appointment along with the others of us. The strange combination of elements both in the moral and physical developments marked this man as a real subject in life's history. Such a subject I would never quit for another when my problem is to describe any thing out of order. Hence I resolved to watch him with a vigilant eye; to lose no occasion to inquire how he fared, and how they fared whom he served. And now, but not by our own fault, but through his own action, we have to cut off his history abruptly. The circuit did not fit him, or else he did not fit the circuit. In his financial strait, he managed to borrow an overcoat of one, money of another, horse and buggy of another, and so far as I have ever learned neither he nor the goods have ever been heard from. He went, as the good people thought, to the place whence he came. Whether there the people all sit, stand, and act alike, I have never learned. Yet in my meditations on this jackanapes, taking away the things he did, through sympathy for the brethren he wronged, I always think he " had n't orter " done it. This whole history goes to show the caution to be used in receiving others who are fond of Church-changing. There are some good men who are honestly convicted and convinced, no doubt, yet there are others who use it as a policy or make-shift to get along through the world.

In the Conference-room.

But I know you want me to go on with my narrative. In the Conference-room was the gravest time with these Methodist preachers. A bishop is in the chair. O what an awe-power he was! True, he was only a man of like passions with others, yet he was seen only once a year, and sometimes even less often in those days, when distances in the West were so great and conveyances so slow. When he did come, however, with some of the brethren, and especially the younger ones who knew but little away from the West, it was like getting a visit from another planet. Perhaps the best order in Conferences was to be found in the West. Business moved regularly on, and without disturbance—not simply on the ground of the awe-power of a presiding bishop, for this did not always happen, but on the ground of Western education, a high self-respect, and its counterpart, a patient consideration of others. The Conference-room is always an exceedingly interesting place to the young preachers. They always go away much improved in both mind and heart.

The Outlook Among the Brethren.

After a few days, the novelty of things having somewhat abated, the principal topics of friendly intercourse having been discussed, conversation turns more in the direction of interest. The old familiar "chum" names are not forgotten. Every one begins to look to an appointment, and yet no one knows where he will be sent. Even the presiding elders work hard to have their districts "well manned," as they call it. Among the preachers you may hear one say, "John, where are you going next year?" "Buck," says another, "what kind of people did you serve last year?" These and similar questions are heard from a rising suspicion or imagination that the questioner has found where he is going the ensuing year. Perhaps a presiding elder has asked some one how he would like to go to Jordan Mills, or how he would like to follow Bill Jones. The poor fellow makes his own inteprtation, and often thinks he is going to the place named by a presiding elder. It is astonishing how many have found out, or think they have found out, where they will be sent the ensuing year. These things, however, are mutable up to the last moment. Many a poor fellow finds things at last neither as he expected nor hoped.

Reading the Appointments.

But at last the inevitable hour arrives that either kills or makes alive. The Conference business is finished, and the appointments are all fixed. A slip of paper is in the bishop's hand that contains the full announcement. He rises deliberately, and before he announces the verdict of the year, from which there can be no appeal, he kindly and fatherly admonishes to heroism, without which no man can achieve a good history—no one can expect a crown. In some parts of his address tears may be seen gathering in the eyes of many. This address is a very useful thing when properly thought and delivered. Many a poor heart that was almost shrinking from the task of a Methodist preacher is encouraged to still endure for the sake of the Master. A stillness now reigns supreme. Hearts are to be tried. The bishop reads the list in slow announcement. Each one, as his own scribe, is trying to write it all down. He wants to know it all, and be able to tell it to the people whom he is appointed to serve; for in the West, with the poor facilities there in those days, months might pass before the published minutes could be distributed. To compensate for this, each one tried to carry the minutes in memory or manuscript.

Look yonder! a face is radiant with pleasure. That one is placed where he would like to go. But look yonder! there is a bowed head. It has unconsciously dropped toward his knees. It is not as he likes; but do not fear—he will go, and before another Conference gathering will find many good fathers and mothers to raise his head, take away his gloom, and bless his soul. But look yonder! no tear is falling. It is the erect form of a noble youth, looking about wistfully, unconscious whether the announcement for him is east, west, north, or south. It matters not; he will go. Under the Master's call he will forsake home endearments, and leave behind a loving mother and a fond sister to lift up before the eyes of men the cross of Christ.

But the last appointment is announced. The curtain drops. Where there was a bowed head it begins to rise up. They begin to wipe away all tears. Then the parting scene is soon over. "Good-by, John; God bless you!" "Good-by, Jake; my good boy, cheer up." "Farewell, Buck; do n't forget to write to me." "Billy, tell ma they have sent me away off yonder, and I cannot come to see her for a year." Away they go. Some east, who had been traveling west; some west who had just traveled east. An army of evangelists, refreshed and newly inspired by their annual gathering, is turned loose again on Satan's kingdom with armor bright; and the "ruler of the darkness of this world" trembles on beholding.

My Assignment—Sorrow—Incidents.

My appointment was to a large mission work, or rather to two missions, in conjunction with a senior brother. The nearest line to reach the work from the seat of the Conference was at least two hundred and fifty miles; but owing to a sad and unexpected circumstance, I was called to go a route of nearly twice this distance. My brother-in-law, who had but recently moved to Texas, had been killed by the accidental falling of a stick of timber. Having received notice of this sad affair, I started for the mission work, but, in sympathy for a sorrowing sister, on this circuitous route.

An incident occurred in my history as I was on my way to this house of sorrow, which I will narrate here because of the surprise it awakened in my mind. I traveled the whole distance from the seat of the Conference to the home of my widowed sister alone—a distance of between two and three hundred miles; much of the way being of a character that awakened in me a spirit of loneliness on account of its solitude. It was principally pine-woods until I reached the neighborhood of the Trinity River, when the pine and sand began to give way to oak and more solid earth. Where I halted for my dinner I was informed there was a short way recently opened across the Trinity River, by which I could save many miles in reaching my destination. I embraced the idea with pleasure, for above all things I wanted to make time. This new way across the Trinity was full of novelty, and proved by no means pleasing to me then. Down, down the Trinity bottom I went for a long distance before I came to the ferry. But one lone traveler had I met that afternoon, and had seen no habitation for several hours. It was a lonesome evening.

On arriving at the ferry, I saw a boat, and it too on the favorable side of the river, but no ferryman. I looked up the river, down the river, across the river, and through the swampy woods, but no human form could I see. In the absence of a horn to blow, I whooped with all my might, but the only responding sounds were the reverberating echoes of my own voice. Night-fall was now approaching, and "I must get out of here" was my immediate resolve. I knew that unless I could have better luck advancing than retreating, the leaves would be my bed and a log my pillow for the night. Though unused to the project of ferrying myself across a river, I nevertheless took off my saddle-bags laid them in the boat, and led in my faithful horse. I then loosed the fastening, and with rope and stick made for the opposite shore. This I could not do by a space of three feet, on account of a stake under water. I threw my saddle-bags on shore, for I carried no *bottle* in them, nor any thing else easily broken. I followed with rope in hand, intending to fasten the boat to shore; but to my surprise, my noble horse, as if impatient and in dread of a crisis, may be through my awkwardness, leaped to shore. My hurry to give him space to light, and the reaction which his spring gave the boat, jerked it loose from my hand. As I saw it receding, I hesitated for a moment to find what I could do. I saw I could do nothing. Wishing no harm might come of it all, I mounted and began to hunt for a place to lodge for the night.

The Surprise of the Night.

On and yet on I went. The dusky eve brought no relief. I was just despairing of finding lodgment for the night when, a little ahead and just off to the left, I discovered a light. It broke graciously on my gloomy mind. What traveler, when late and weary, would not thank God for light and a home for the night. "Hello!" rang my voice on the night air as from a gladdened heart. A figure appears; another, and another. They are Indians, as veritable Indians as I had ever seen. But, however, thought I, it may not be so bad after all, although I have never heard there were any Indians in these parts. I made known that I was a weary traveler, wanted lodging for the night, and food for my horse. I was permitted to alight, but got ill fare both for myself and horse. After eating a little of such as they furnished me, I sat by the little fire they had kindled, for the evening was cool. To my great surprise, one of them became very inquisitive. Reticence is the general character of the Indian, but this one, either from the promptings of an abnormal nature or from some manifestations growing out of my surprise, became very free to interrogate me. He seemed to understand the geography of the State. "What is your name?" said he. This I gave. "Where do you live?" I gave him the place where I had been living. "Where have you been?" I gave him the place. "Where are you going?" I answered, naming the counties in which my mission work lay. "In the cattle business?" "Not extensively," said I. "Well, what you come 'way round here for?" Now, I admit I was traveling circuitously awkward to the mind of one who did not fully understand my intentions; but this was more than I could stand even from a *red* man, who showed culture enough as a host not to have put such questions to the traveler. I turned my eyes on him with the determination of true manhood, and addressed him as follows: "Sir, you have taken me in for the night, and as a traveler I claimed you as my host. You have violated the courtesy which properly exists between us in the relation we sustain of host and traveler. Whether it arises from your ignorance or grossly from your heart, I cannot tell. As it relates to myself, you shall know who I am. I am what is called a Methodist circuit-rider. I have been attending an Annual Conference of the preachers, and am on this circuitous route to visit a recently widowed and sorely afflicted sister; after which I shall travel and preach on the mission work to which I am assigned. You will now, sir, please show me where I may rest for the night." He did not look pleased at all, though he uttered not a word. Others were present, but they said nothing; they looked as though they did not know how to take it, or else did not understand what was up.

The cabin had two rooms, and I was shown to the other. In it there was a place cut out for a chimney which had never been built. The head of my bed was immediately by that. I blew out the sort of burning wick with which I had been supplied—taking care first, however, to reconnoiter the room, and to evade as far as possible any uneasiness should any one in any conceivable way be watching me. I took some old wrecks of benches, that for some cause were lying in the room, and propped the door; that made it troublesome and noisy for any one to enter that way. This left me no place to guard except the niche in the wall cut for a future fire-place. I lay down on the bed with my plans all matured. I could not suppress the uneasiness of the hour. I do not remember that I prayed; I rather think I did not. I was anxious for any thing that was intended; I wanted it to come off without delay, result in whatever way it might. I felt a kind of readiness, and lay awake for a long time waiting and expecting. I even snored aloud to induce them, if any thing was intended, to begin the action. But the dead stillness of the night indicated repose all around. I became much wearied through watching, so much so that unconsciously and unintentionally I sunk away into sound sleep. When I awoke the sun was giving occasional glimpses through the trees, and there was a hum of voices around. All went well, and probably all was meant well; yet I take no pleasure in such experiences, and do not desire to have them repeated in my history.

My Bereaved Sister.

When I arrived at my sister's I felt a considerable weariness through the journey I had made; but this was soon forgotten by the spectacle presented by the little family. They had been in Texas but a short time, only a few days, when the sad calamity already mentioned befell them. Far away from friends and loved ones left behind, and having had but a short time to make acquaintances in the West—she herself apparently blooming in youth, yet with eyes declining to sadness and a face marked with care and sorrow; around her five unconscious innocents, going or wanting to go wherever she went. They often in their prattling way mentioned the name *papa*, but never without bringing tears to the eyes of the sorrowing mother. Circumstances all seemed to meet in a way that truly made this a house of sorrow—even such as our Saviour would have visited had it been in Palestine, and in those days when he personally walked with men. She herself was young, and ardently devoted to her husband; just arrived in a new country, and far away from old home and friends; the unfortunate and unexpected death of her husband; the five little children around her, whose memories were full of papa's looks and care. This sad picture to this day has never left my memory. It became fastened in me with a hold that time, with its changes, can never erase. She had enough of this world's goods for all necessary comfort, but no measure of these things could compensate for the vacant chair, nor could they lift the load from the heart. It was one of those heavy burdens a mortal here below has sometimes to bear. Here I became convinced that sorrow can plow his deepest furrows without the aid of pinching poverty. I have visited many a house of sorrow since; but were I a painter and desired to paint young widowhood in sorrow, my pencil would naturally fall on the scene here so feebly pictured to the view. There would be in it none of the squalidness of poverty, yet there would be in it the eyes and face which show how things lay about the heart. I remained several days here. My dear sister appeared a little improved and more resigned when I left. I saw, however, that sorrow was cutting deep tracks that would remain on a beautiful face like a scar through life. I endeavored to show her the advantages she had over some widows, and exhorted her not to sink too deeply into a state of melancholy. I bid good-by deeply impressed in my own soul. I dropped a tear, trusted God, and started for my assigned mission work.

Horse Swapping.

I was now anxious to get to the missions and see what I could do for the salvation of souls. I had heard that it was a little dangerous on the missions on account of the Indians. I began to think my horse was hardly suited for such a work. I likewise always believed that God would only do for us what we could not do for ourselves. Therefore, I thought it prudent to try and get better mounted. On my way I stopped for a night's lodging with a Mr. Harris, a jovial, pleasant, good-natured man toward the traveler. I made known to him my missionary work, and the fact that I thought a man traveling such a work, on account of the danger, should be well mounted. In this he entirely agreed with me, and in his jovial, pleasant way said: "Why, I have got the very horse you need for such a work.

You look like a clever young man, and I would hate to hear of your being scalped. I think I can set you up just right for your dangerous mission work. In the morning I will show him to you, and if you wish to trade I will give you a good bargain."

Now, this Mr. Harris was one of those men peculiarly tempered in that way, in which a horse never passed by unless he looked at him with an earnest gaze. He looked at the form and observed the gaits of all horses. He formed his opinions of horses readily, and I think seldom erred. He doubtless then knew all about my horse in the stable, though I was unconscious of it. However, that night in answering him I said: "Very well, sir; any righteous trade in which I can mount myself better for the mission work to which I am assigned I shall certainly be willing to make, and shall regard it as a favor."

The morning light broke upon me much refreshed. In due time the talked-of horse was brought to my inspection. "How old is your horse, Mr. Harris?" said I. Said he: "I am a member of the Presbyterian Church, and I think you might say Brother Harris." "Very well," said I; "then, Brother Harris, how old is your horse?" "He is eight years old," said he. "That, Brother Harris," said I, "is a very clever age. Your horse is neither too young nor too old for durability." "Look in his mouth," said he. "Ah! Brother Harris, as to that," said I, "I shall have to depend on your statement, for I know nothing of that science." "Well," said he, "there is the horse. I have told you that he is eight years old. Tommy, get on him and show his gaits. See, he moves cleverly in three or four ways, but that fox-trot is the best for regular traveling. I'll venture when mounted on that horse the scalping-knife will never get near to your head, for that horse has speed. An Indian never owned a horse that could catch him. Now, I will tell you what I will do. Though my horse is larger than yours, as well formed and better gaited, you can ride off either one you want." I thought a moment; and yet it seemed like there was no use in thinking, for Brother Harris's horse, in my judgment, was the best for me in the mission work, though I knew mine was a good horse of his class. "I believe, Brother Harris," said I, "that I will ride off your horse and leave mine with you." "All right," said he, "but I hate very much to see Pompey go." Now, I hated to leave my faithful George behind; but I regarded him in good hands, and was sure he would be kindly treated. Away I went on "Pompey" for the missions; a noble-spirited fellow, indeed. Why, surely he is all that Brother Harris represented, and even more. It is a blessed thing to meet with good men, thought I, and was no longer thinking of my horse, and had ceased watching his gaits. I suppose I had traveled five miles when the manner of my horse called my attention to him again. He was not getting along well; he was sadly failing. At ten miles he was fearfully under; all his sprightliness was gone, and all his nimbleness of foot. His story is soon told. He was a broken-down steed, eight years old, to be sure, but how much older perhaps Mr. Harris himself did not know. He was an old horse which in his young days kept his spirit for a day, but now in age, pampered for a cheat, could endure for only an hour or two.

Do you ask me what I think of Mr. Harris? I will tell you. I think he had a good mother and some good brothers, for several of them were in the ministry. I think his wife was a good woman, and that all their children that take after their mother will be honorable and good. I think he had many good neighbors who never told falsehoods by suppressing part of the truth. I think the Presbyterian Church to which he belonged is about as good as any of the Churches, and that thousands of her members will by and by reach the sunlit shores of the blissful future, where there is no necessity for Methodist circuit-riders to swap horses with Presbyterian farmers. Now, you are bound to say that all of these are good opinions, and yet they are all I have to say of my host, Mr. Harris.

How I Finally Got Mounted for the Mission Work.

Now, I owned a little ranch stocked with a few horses. This ranch lay in the direction of the mission work to which I was assigned. On it lived a friend. Finally I arrived at my ranch and explained to my friend how I came to be afoot. This friend was fond of a joke, laughed heartily at my mishap, and said: "I know exactly how I could suit myself in this emergency, and I think it would suit you." "My friend," said I, "that is the very kind of talk I wish to hear just now, but I am sure there is no horse on this ranch that will answer my purpose." "No, no," said he, "but would you have any objections to riding a race horse?" "Well," said I, "that depends upon the circumstances. If it is to ride him on the track, or to train him for the races, I would most seriously object on the ground of the morality involved; but if it is for getting away from the Indians, I would regard myself happy to be so well mounted." "Well, I will tell you," said he, "Mr. Scruggs, over in town, has a black race-horse of pretty good turn to be managed, and wants to trade him for a work-horse. I think that bay horse of yours, with a white spot in his face, will suit him. If you can get that black horse, my word for it, you will be well mounted." "Thank you, my friend," said I; "to-morrow I must of necessity attend to a little business in town. I will ride Handle," for that was the name of the horse to which my friend referred, "and I will see whether my horse suits Mr. Scruggs." "You need not fear on that score," said he, "for I rode him to town the other day, and he asked me if that was a good work-horse. He said that he was done with racing, and wanted a work-horse." Accordingly, on the next day, I rode Handle into town and rode out on the Scruggs black race-horse. All trading was fairly done, and Mr. Scruggs, as I afterward learned, was pleased with Handle. I do not know what was the former name of my black horse, but I named him George; and a sensible, faithful horse he proved to me.

It is astonishing how a horse becomes attached to

his master, under kind treatment. There were never better friends than George and I. He seemed to depend on me as much as I depended on him. If ever he cut a caper a little tormenting to his master, he seemed immediately to repent by showing a fondling disposition. He was to me what Bucephalus was to Alexander—a dear horse indeed. This little tribute of respect I pay here because it is due to that faithful old servant. He was much attached to his master, as well as his master to him.

On the Missions—My New Title.

Now, being fully equipped, in the month of November, facing a stiff Texas Norther, I started for my first appointment. This was in a little village but recently sprung up. I arrived on the evening before my appointment to preach. It was soon whispered around that the *new* preacher had come. Here, for the first time, I was called "Parson." It did sound so strange and queer to me. It is a little word, and to be known by such an epithet appeared to dry up the fountain of my pleasure, especially when it was the manner of all whom I met to shower it on me. "Good-morning, parson. Well, parson, they have sent you to a big work. How do you think you can stand it out here on these large missions, parson? You have a fine-looking horse, parson; do you want to swap him?" Off to one side, the same uncomfortable word could be heard ringing on the morning and evening air. Listen: "The parson is a young-looking man. Do you know what State the parson is from? Don't you think the parson is pretty good-looking?" "O dear!" thought I, "does the Methodist circuit-rider have to stand all this?"

I have given the foregoing specimens, as indicative of the manner in which the new handle to my name was used. How much more preferable is Mister, or Brother. How I wished for the day when this uncouth, degenerate epithet should be lost to the world!

My First Sermon on the Missions — Singing — "Brother Jesse" — Frontier Meeting-house.

But now the day, the hour arrived in which I was to make my first effort publicly, as a circuit-rider. I had preached three or four times, to be sure, before going to Conference, but then not with the pressure of responsibility I now felt. I went to the house of just the character all frontiersmen first have, and of which they are always proud—a house of about eighteen by twenty-four feet, with board window-shutters to close off the cold; a door cut just anywhere a man may happen first to strike; a puncheon floor, and split logs mounted on legs for benches. A house to be used on all occasions, public or otherwise; for it was never known to have a key. In it the preacher preached, the boys held their polemics, the master taught, the clown exhibited, and the immigrant camped. On Sunday it looked a little tidy, or otherwise, according to the weather and the manner in which it had just previously been occupied. But having been a frontiersman two or three years, I could endure almost any thing, whether I liked it or not.

I took my position in one corner, the observed of all observers. I wanted to sing. I would have given any thing to sing well; but this had been an accomplishment neglected in my education, mainly because my voice was hard to train. Said I, "Will some one please give us a voluntary song?" They looked at one another, but gave no response to me. I heard one, however, say: "Jesse, lead out. You can beat any one singing round here, Uncle Tom says." But neither Jesse nor any one else led out. I fully appreciated the responsibility of the young preacher. I could in a sort of way sing a few of the old familiar hymns. I sung one of these in the sort of way I was able, and as best I could—a few old ladies throwing in their interludes whenever their ideas and mine agreed. We sung it through. It sometimes awakened looks of surprise, but more frequently pleasant smiles. This converted Jesse. He was no longer ashamed nor afraid to sing. Indeed he lost no time, for scarcely had mine and the old ladies' voices died away when he snatched up another hymn, in a voice far more stentorian and musical, and in which many joined. I felt heartily ashamed of myself, yet I was glad Jesse lived, and had the power through song of linking himself so close to me. "Jesse," thought I, "I will make you a leader here." I then looked down on my text while the singing went on.

It was not long before I was up before the people announcing my text: "Choose you this day whom ye will serve." (Joshua xxiv. 15.) I regard that and all similar texts to this day very well suited to beginners in the ministry. They are at liberty to dwell and comment much on the appertaining history, and thereby very much evade the obstructions of the gospel—a business pertaining to riper years and a deeper acquaintance with the word. I closed my sermon, as I thought, very well. At least I felt a pleasure, a calm satisfaction, and a full determination to go on with the ministry. I was about to dismiss the congregation, when some one suggested the propriety of an evening service at the residence of Brother Daily. As it was now my business to preach, and as I felt flushed with victory, and a joyful complacency over my sermon just finished, I took pleasure in making the appointment accordingly.

The Evening Service and the Fruits it Bore.

In the shades of the evening, the people began to assemble at Brother Daily's, and I among them. The veritable Jesse was there; thanks to his good soul! My text on this occasion was the first Psalm. I felt a consciousness that I would succeed. I counted on nothing else. I am satisfied, however, that my reliance was too much in the virtue of my own powers. I did not feel the humility necessary to successful preaching. I began—I thought I was doing well—I soon discovered myself keyed too high in voice. The thought embarrassed me—I was running at too many knots an hour. I tried to work myself into more deliberation. I felt a heavy pressure. I imagined my congregation sympathized. It was a shock on my nerves. I could not recover. A film came over my eyes. Things looked dark around me. I found myself stammering. I knew I was stumbling. I would retreat but for the disgrace. I tried to rally, but I could not recover. I would, but I could n't. I tried, but I did n't. I was talking away, but I did n't see the point. I was up, but I wanted to be down. I was there, but I wanted to be away. I would quit, but it was too soon. I would go on, but I had nothing to say. "O how shall I get out of this sad trouble?" thought I. Just then—O fortunate indeed!—my eyes, through the film of my understanding, fell on the noble Jesse. O what a relief! Sitting down in the deepest sympathy for myself, mortified and slain, in the deepest humility, I said, "Brother Jesse, please sing."

Jesse was ready. In a twinkling he was at it, as if making up for all lost time. Thus it went—Jesse sung. Some joined in with him; others looked about. I was sad. But by and by the song is finished. The service is concluded with prayer, and the congregation is dismissed. I staid with Brother Daily.

O what a fix I was in! The people were talking about things as usual. I wondered why they were not talking about my sermon on the first Psalm. "How could they be thinking about any thing else?" was the wonder with me. I wanted some one to talk to me about my sermon and failure. It would give me a chance to apologize. I was willing for anybody to call it a failure. It would be foolish to render any other verdict. I felt ashamed to introduce the subject myself. Even Jesse, for whom I was feeling a warm affection, was gone. "Ah!" thought

I, "I am resolved what I will do; when the morning comes, I will saddle up George, and I will turn his head off these missions. I will not stultify myself with this kind of doing. Before everybody finds how big a fool I am, I will retire where my friend is on my little ranch, and either in comparative obscurity pursue the avocation of a small stockman, or else go to the law again." With this resolve firmly fixed in my mind, I retired, not to rest, but to ponder human life with its uprisings and its downgoings.

In an adjoining room, several young people were engaged in conversation. I heard my name called, or rather the inevitable "Parson" I have already mentioned. I laid my ear close to the wall and listened, if ever mortal listened here below. I wanted to hear the verdict. I was anxious to hear their sport. Hush! listen! "The parson looks young, does n't he?" "Yes, he is just starting in the ministry. The sermon he preached to-night is good for a young preacher. He'll make his mark." "Is it possible?" thought I. Yes, these are only a few of the private sentiments I heard that night through the board wall between us. My whole being became revolutionized by this providence. I had been "cast down, but not destroyed." "No, I will not play the truant. I will plow furrows through these missions. I have the respect of the people remaining with me yet, and I will not forsake them. I will go, by the grace of God; I will go in prayer and in tears; I will go in courage and in meekness; I will go because the Master calls, and his providences are over me;

and as I go I will preach the riches of Heaven's grace to the comfort of every heart." I always since have looked back to the struggle I had that night with pleasure. I learned in it how the Lord wants his ministers to be of humble mind, and how his providences work to the profit of the soul and to usefulness in his kingdom. Again, I often think how narrowly I escaped the danger. Had I deserted my post, as I resolved, there is no telling the ruin into which I might have fallen. Under the new reflections awakened in me, my rest became balmy and refreshing.

Area of the Missions—Meeting with the Senior Preacher.

These missions to which we were assigned, two in number, extended over a vast territory—bordering on Red River, and extending southward in the State about one hundred miles, with an average breadth of forty miles. They had been traveled before, but not unitedly as now. Every year their area became increased to the full extent of the westward settlements.

The senior preacher with whom I was assigned I met within a few days after my first experience on the work. He was a man that took life easy, was well adapted to Western life, easily accommodated himself to circumstances, and had been for several years a missionary among the Indians. He was a man of good soul, devout, but not sufficiently cultivated so as to form a man of manners, constituting a good model for the young man to lay off a pattern by.

The manner of arranging the mission work for the year was to make the "round" of it a six weeks appointment. Inasmuch as we were without a plan, it lay in such a condition as necessitated a reörganization of it altogether. Hence, he took one-half of it and gave to me the other half, each to organize his half in three weeks and submit a plan to the other. This we did, and we were but little together during the year. Following each other's plans of organization, we each traveled the entire work in six weeks, always three weeks apart, and giving every congregation a service every three weeks, statedly. So that in three weeks the work was fully organized, subject, however, to some changes which followed as our acquaintance with the work became more thorough. Wherever we went we left an appointment to be back ourselves in six weeks, and each for the other in three weeks. Many places needed the gospel which had not received it. I soon discovered the progressive character of Methodism. No other denomination of Christians was pushing so much to the front and with such persistent energy.

Character of the People.

Wherever I went I was kindly taken in; and though a stranger, the comforts of the cabin or camp-fire were cheerfully divided, and to me was given a share. The people were generally poor, but exceedingly kind. They had not received much of the gospel, yet were disposed to be religious. They were rather uncouth in dress and manners, but they had good hearts and stout courage. Some had herds of cattle and horses that subsisted on the spontaneous pasturage of the country. Generally, the soil was not much cultivated. To take them all in all, they were as clever people as you will find anywhere, but greatly lacking in advantages. If they could afford no accommodation, it was not for the want of a heart, but of the means. They were inured to hardships; never boasted of what they had; never complained of their want. They were just the class of people to go forward in a new country. They prepared the way for complete civilization, and stood between it and the red man, the buffalo and the bear. They were a pioneering people, courted danger, loved the freedom of frontier life, and moved on ahead of all general improvement. With them neither fashion nor diet changed the year round. Their removals were all toward the West. They complained of being hampered when the settlement became a little dense, and that the range for their stock was wasting away. Such was the character of the people on the missions, and such was the character of most of the border people.

EXPECTATION BLASTED—DISGUST.

On the eastern border of these missions lived a Methodist minister—a man of considerable experience in the ministry. I congratulated myself when I was approaching his section of the country. I counted on having a pleasant and profitable night with him. I thought he could give me much information about the missions such as I needed. Besides, I hoped to get much information from him about how to study, prepare sermons, preach, and conduct myself generally as a young minister; for I reminded myself of a young bird in its nest, and while I was ready and willing to apply myself, I was anxious to receive from my seniors any crumbs of instruction which might fall from their lips. I did not find, however, in this brother such as I would, and consequently I failed to realize in his house the pleasure I anticipated. He was quite ignorant of the missions to which I was sent, and, as I thought, of missionary work generally. Instead of being an exemplar generally, he picked his teeth at the table with his fork—which act, under your training, dear mother, was so disgusting to me that I never felt disposed to repeat my visit at that house again. Yet, as my patience was so exercised in sermonizing, I thought surely this brother could help me a little, and consequently I asked him for advice. This he was very ready to give. Said he: "I would recommend that you commit three or four of Wesley's sermons and preach them. Out of these, by hunting texts to suit by properly dividing up, you may make yourself eight or ten; and that is about as many as a man needs. Whenever he preaches he can preach one of these; but frequently an exhortation will answer every purpose."

Which disgusted me most—this instruction, or the act at the table—I am not able to say. The whole of it was mortifying to my flesh and repulsive to my nature. "Are we to regard all manhood clean gone?" thought I. "Are we to class ourselves with plagiarists, parrots, and mimics—only speaking the words of others—and when we die leave the world just where we found it?" "No, my brother," said I, "your advice I cannot take; I cannot be recreant to the instruction of a mother who always exhorted me to true manhood. I am no rogue; I will not plagiarize as you recommend. 'Sink or swim, live or die, survive or perish,' go up or down, preach or fail, I will make my own sermons." The brother, upon this announcement, delivered earnestly and emphatically, appeared at a loss for a reply. I must say such a spontaneity was not usual with me then. It only broke like a bursting dam from my mind and heart under a keen sense of disgust.

I have since known a few other preachers who repudiated self-reliance and depended on others. But I am satisfied that it would be best for all to spend more time in investigating than in committing. There is more of true manhood in it. It is a blessing to have a good memory; but if it works the evil in the person possessing it of plagiarizing and of depending on it altogether, it proves a curse. Wesley's, Watson's, and other sermons I would by no means undervalue. They may be profitable in a reading course, but in form and style are not best adapted to reach men's hearts in this age. Young men should be trained to investigate, grapple with problems, look into the philosophy of the people's minds, and from close thinking, more than from memory, build their sermons in that form which obtains the best hearing and rebukes the most present evils.

BUNCOMBE COUNTY ILLUSTRATED—FURTHER COMMENT.

I had not been on the missions many days when one day in dusky eve I came upon the residence of Brother Jones, a Methodist, and a farmer away ahead of any I had seen, so far as I had yet traveled the work. He reminded me much of my boyhood days. He was the owner of a dozen or more slaves, and between him and them existed perfect harmony. Sister Jones was the most motherly woman whom I had met. Brother Jones, Sister Jones, and one single daughter, comprised the family of *whites*. The other children were married and gone to themselves. I was kindly requested to make their house my head-quarters, or my home, while on the work. This I very gratefully accepted; and though I knew I could not spend much time with them, yet there was a place I could call home, and a good woman whom in heart I could call mother. The taste displayed by this family, their lines of thought, and their conversation, were congenial to my nature, and tended to intellectual and spiritual elevation. Now, this well-to-do farmer lived in a very rugged portion of the country. It presented just such a face as is least pleasing to the eye. He lived on a hill, yet from his residence vision was soon eclipsed by other hills and brush-wood in every direction. He never saw the sun rise, and just as unfrequently saw it set. Between him and the hills around were deep-cut ravines, and along their margins could be seen corners of his fields. The line of his fencing took direction according to the shape of the hills and the course of the rivulets meandering between. It made no difference in what direction you found yourself from his residence, there was but one way of mounting the hill to get to it. You always approached it by a single way, and with much circumlocution. Indeed, it was a wonder to me why such a selection for a home should be made in a new country at so early a day, when immigrants had such choice, and especially by one who was financially—like Saul, son of Kish, was physically—head and shoulders above all the rest.

"Brother Jones," said I, "where are you from?" "From Buncombe county, North Carolina," said he. "Well," said I, "considering your finances and possibilities, it seems very strange to me that you, after traveling all the way here from the Atlantic coast, should make such a selection as this for a home. What inspiration drove you to this, Brother Jones?" Said he: "I will give you a sketch of my history, and then you will understand how it has come to pass as you find it. For many years, while in my Buncombe home, I had from time to time been hearing beautiful things of Texas lands and of the beautiful prairies. Long before I left my Buncombe home I had a desire to see and live in a country where hills were scarce. At last my desire ripened into my removal to the West. When I saw the beautiful, gradually undulating prairies of Texas, with their rich soil and grazing herds, I thought every now and then that I would stop, drive a stake, find the owner, and make a purchase. But I went on until I, from some cause which I do not understand, paid out my money for this place; and since I have improved it and looked over it, I find no place in Texas that looks more like my old Buncombe homestead than this." "Ah! Brother Jones," said I, "we understand it; there is no helping human nature; we naturally love the old homestead; we think sometimes that we do not, and quit it in disgust. Yet we want the orchard in the same direction, the barn and the spring. We want a like appearance of hills and woods, and brooks and vales. On account of these we sometimes leave the old home, seeking another view and a better fortune; but as we settle again, our old love returns, and ere we are aware we find ourselves, like you, in another Buncombe home. Love of home, like patriotism, dwells inherent."

Now, there are many men in the world like Brother Jones. It may not be the prominent old homestead in every case; yet they have left the dear old home and gone far away, seeking a better fortune. Ere they are aware they have lost opportunities and paid out their money, and when they cast their eyes about have no advantages over the old homestead. I was traveling some years ago far to the south-west of the missions. The ground was parched, the day was hot, and I was longing to find water for the comfort of both myself and my horse; the country all along presenting no strange contrast with that about Brother Jones's, but every little rivulet-bed was dry. After several hours' fatigue, thirst, and weariness, I finally came to a habitation. Here I was in the midst of hills, woods, and naked knobs. I was just about to congratulate myself on drawing near to the habitation when my pleasure began to wane, for my eyes had fallen on the historical "sled and barrel" that indicated "water scarce." A number of pleasant and seemingly happy faces in the way of children were soon exhibited to the traveler, who rarely passed through that country, and among them the genial proprietor, a man perhaps forty years of age. "How do you do, sir?" said I to the proprietor, whom I had now approached, and whose face, being all sunshine, indicated that he was by no means a man of moody turn. "Very well, I thank you. How is yourself?" "Thirsty, sir, thirsty, both myself and horse. What is the chance for a slake?" "Pretty good for yourself," said he, "but not for your horse; my dependence is on that barrel." "I am a little sorry for my horse's sake," said I; "however, sir, I will try and make the most of it, and thank you. But what country are you from, my friend?" "From Maryland," said he. "How long have you been here?" "About six years." "Have you any neighbors?" "Yes, sir." "How far away are they?" "About four miles." "Have you any churches or school-houses near you?" "None nearer than eight miles." "How far do you haul your water?" "About four miles these dry times." "Have you any preaching near you?" "We have had it a few times at neighbor Ruskin's since I have lived here." "What denomination?" "The Methodist." "I see you have some clever-looking boys. Are you educating them?" He gave me a wondering, sorrowful look and made no reply. Said I: "My friend, I think you have come a long way to make a mistake. Look well to those clever-looking boys. Thank you, sir, for the water." I bid him good-by, and rode on in my meditations.

Brother Jones Again—My Lesson from Sister Jones.

But I must come back to my good Brother Jones. The next morning as I was saddling George, Brother Jones came to me and asked if I knew it was a little hazardous to travel the missions. I told him that I supposed it was on account of marauding bands of Indians. I further stated that I would thank him for any advice he could give me. By this time we were in his house again, and ready for a little talk, as I intended before I left. Sister Jones had been watching my maneuvering, and had all things ready for a parting prayer before I left. She placed a chair by the stand on which the Bible always lay, and nodded to her husband, who immediately invited me to pray with them before I mounted my horse. I had just prayed with them before breakfast, and now to crowd another prayer immediately on breakfast appeared to me to be wedging breakfast pretty close on both sides. It partook richly, as I thought, of the Presbyterian style of grace—a blessing of consecration upon and thanks after. I remember once since in my life when our Annual Conference and a Presbyterian Synod were held contemporaneously in the same town, several Presbyterian ministers and I had got assignment to board at the same house, the proprietor of which was a Presbyterian himself. Very unexpectedly to me, and perhaps unfortunately, before retiring from the table I was called on to return thanks. I have always doubted whether I made a good "hit." It was one of the acts of my life done in blindness, and I have never been able to recall the service. I may hear from it yet some day, for no doubt but that it was good enough to impress the memories of my good Presbyterian friends and the polite proprietor. But I prayed immediately after breakfast, according to invitation, with Brother Jones, Sister Jones, young Miss Jones, and a few of the servants who were remaining about the house. One verse in the lesson I read impressed me deeply: "Pray without ceasing." I never thought afterward that I could crowd my prayers too much. Said I: "Sister Jones, I am glad you arranged for prayer before I left. I believe it has done me good." I then referred her to the text, "Pray without ceasing." "Why," said she, "my good young brother, have you not been praying with the families with whom you stopped, just before leaving them?" "No, Sister Jones," said I thoughtfully. "Suppose there is no arrangement made, and I am not invited?" Said she: "My young brother, you must pray in the families of our people, and it matters not how often; at least, always leave a parting blessing. I put out the Bible through custom. I know no other way. Ah!" said she, continuing, "you have a high office now. Do thou only magnify it. You are to mold not only your own character as a minister of Christ, but you are to help mold the character of our people. Whenever you find the custom wrong, change it for something better. Do it by all means. Do it in a gentlemanly, Christian way. Nobody will fall out with you for it; but they will love you the more. Just keep yourself in a devotional spirit, and you will succeed; you need not fear. When Mr. Jones and I were young and in our Carolina home, I remember well in pleasant memory how Bishop Andrew, then young like ourselves and you are now, often visited our home. He was a blessing to our house, and never left without a parting prayer. He taught me how to keep my Bible always ready." This was enough. I was encouraged. I resolved to pray wherever I went, and above all to leave a parting benediction.

"Now," said Brother Jones, "I propose to talk to you about the missions before you leave. But I see you have no gun. I think it might serve you a good purpose." "Brother Jones," said I, "do you think that I am preparing to fight the Indians? Do you see that black horse out yonder? That is a regularly trained race-horse; quick to start, yet easily guided and checked. I traded for him on purpose for the missions. I believe in building storm retreats, in using lightning-rods, in getting out from under falling trees, and in riding a fleet horse when exposed to the Indians. I incorporate in my theology this principle—that we are to use all means in our power for safety, and that God interposes only when we are reduced to extremity."

"That is all good philosophy and good theology;

yet you do not go far enough with it," said Brother Jones. "Do you not know that nothing is more pleasing to the Indians than fleeing away from them, and that nothing gives them better opportunity? They seize upon this advantage readily and eagerly. More people have been scalped in this way than in any other. On open, even ground, from what you say, you would not be caught unless by accident; and yet accidents, you know, do sometimes happen. Do you not know that in the brush-wood and on some ground your race-horse would not have much advantage over a horse slower in his motion; indeed, none over a trained Indian pony. Again, it is characteristic of the Indian to press his foe to the life when fleeing, on the ground that he is always impressed that only unarmed men flee away. But an Indian's life is as sweet to him as yours is to you, and he is even more careful to preserve it. Whenever he sees a white man he hides himself away. The sight of a gun or the dreaded six-shooter are both terrors alike to him. Now, in case of accident, or on the ground of standing, you must have something to defend yourself with, or you may lose your life; and if lose it you must, it will be a pleasant recollection to your friends that you died with your Bible in your pocket, your gun in your hand, and your face to the foe." "Well, Brother Jones," said I, "that is all very beautiful, and I see I did not go far enough with my philosophy. I believe I ought to have a gun, or at least a six-shooter, which is far more convenient." "But," said Brother Jones, "you must not think the Indians are going to invade the settlements for the avowed purpose of killing the people, for that would be war indeed. They do, however, I believe, have some old prejudices, and are ready to be revenged at any moment. They may make mistakes in such a case; and when laboring under disappointment, they are not very careful about it any way. Their character is to find revenge; and if they cannot find the objects of their hate, they slay the innocent. But their present purpose is to steal horses. They sometimes come as marauding bands into my own vicinity. Not long since they carried out about one hundred head of horses. I believe your mission work extends to Red River, and as far west as there are settlements, which is at least forty miles farther on the frontier. I would advise you by all means to be soldierly, and make the full round; and if you will accept it, I will lend you a six-shooter." "I thank you, Brother Jones, for all this information, and for the loan of the six-shooter. I will get mine which I have below and return yours in about six weeks." "If you do n't get scalped, and turn it over to the Indians," interluded he, in a half witty and half tempting way. To this I made no reply. "Now mind you," said he, "for while the Indians may not be after you, yet if you happen on them, they may try to put you out of the way. They slip in slyly, and will leave no living witnesses of their presence if they can help it when on one of their marauding excursions."

An Illustrative Anecdote.

I rose to my feet, buckled Brother Jones's six-shooter around me, and cast my eyes over toward Sister Jones, thinking may be time was up for prayers again; but she gave no token to Brother Jones, and I did not insist. Good-by, Brother Jones; good-by, Sister Jones; good-by, Miss Russie; good-by to old Aunt Silva, the negro nurse. Out again on George, and toward the front. I did not go out, however, with all the notions of an old Baptist pioneer preacher, of whom I have heard, in the State of Missouri. To be sure, we were both a sort of circuit-riders. He carried his gun and I a six-shooter, but he with more notions than myself. His wife observed him one day over-anxious about his gun, and carefully preparing it before starting on his pioneer round of preaching. She, having drank in the Baptist sentiment of God's providences, thought the old gentlemen, her husband, was unnecessarily troubling himself over things appointed and inevitable at any rate, said: "Why, Mr. Glannell, do you trouble yourself so much about your gun? Do you not know that if the Indians come upon you, and your time has come, the gun will do you no good?" "O yes," said Mr. Glannell, "that is all very true if *my* time has come—I understand all that perfectly; but see here, Becca, suppose I come upon an Indian and *his* time has come, what could I do without the gun?" Now, I did not have so many notions, nor did I in arming myself have my religion so interwoven in the act. I did not at all carry a six-shooter to visit Heaven's decrees on the Indians, but simply for personal safety, believing, as I do, that God requires us to avail ourselves of all possible means for the preservation of our lives.

A Portion of Country Described.

I had now entered the Upper Cross Timbers, a belt of woods dipping down into the State from Red River, for a long distance. These woods are about sixteen miles wide, but not regularly that width. They are composed mainly of post-oak and blackjack, all of which is a dwarf growth in comparison with these sturdy oaks of Kentucky. In many places this woodland district presents a half-open appearance, so that in the main it is not difficult to traverse. Here and there mats of prairies may be seen, especially on the lower grounds and valleys—except at the very margins of the streams, where the brush-wood is very dense in most places. Here I found wild-turkeys very abundant, and in the unsettled portions not much afraid of man. Deer, bear, and panthers were denizens of these woods. The people here rarely ever lived remote from each other. They formed, as they called them, settlements, or neighborhoods. They did this as a necessary defense against the Indians. If their horses should be stolen, they could sometimes in a few hours collect together in order to give chase, inflict the deserving penalty on the miscreants, and recover their stolen property. These people had sent out parties among the buffalo just before my arrival. The proceeds of the hunt had been divided around. Wherever I went, I saw buffalo-rugs, and on the table dried, or, as they called it, "jerked buffalo-flesh."

Coffee—How I Remedied an Evil.

In the West, I had always up to this time been used to coffee, especially for breakfast; but in traveling and organizing this mission work, I found that I not only had to deny myself, but that compelling circumstances denied me of sinless luxuries. I had heard old ladies say if they did not get their cup of coffee for breakfast they would have the headache. One morning, while traveling as usual, a very severe and unexpected headache had come on me. I was at a loss to account for it. I thought I was going to be suddenly sick, and was in mental distress about it; for above all things I wanted health, and to make this my first year in the ministry a useful one. Coming up to a house about eleven o'clock, I got permission to stop awhile, on the ground of being sick. The lady of the house was very kind, and when I made known that I was a preacher, sent out on the border of the settlements, she made many inquiries about whether I was accustomed to such spells and how long I had been unwell. I answered her promptly, as best I could. She asked me if my diet was not different from that I had been accustomed to. I told her it was, but that I had felt no inconvenience on that score. She said: "Do you drink coffee?" I answered: "I do when I am well." She said again: "Have you had coffee since you have been traveling the missions?" Said I: "I have, except for breakfast to-day." Said she, in a knowing way: "Jennie, put on the coffee-pot. I know what is the matter with this young preacher." Coffee was soon made. I drank and was soon relieved.

When I had to confess this physical weakness, I felt very much ashamed of myself. I felt much humbled, but thanked God that my malady was so slight. I thanked this kind lady for her attention, and thought she deserved a much better reward than I could give. I spoke to her husband and said: "My dear sir, if it meets with your approbation, we will offer prayer in your family before we leave. Said he: "Why, a preacher has never been with us before, and we have been here two years. We do not belong to the Church, but we believe in praying. Certainly, pray with us." I did pray, and with a full soul. When I left, my most pious benedictions remained with that family. My mind went back in fond memory of good Sister Jones, who had inspired me with this courage.

Several times I through necessity suffered with this wretched headache. I found a remedy, however, and at small cost. The saddle-bags are the treasury department of the Methodist circuit-rider. Down among my books and papers, one day, I slipped a small sack of parched coffee. Not many days passed away before I had the opportunity of testing its virtue. Breakfast being served without coffee, I had not gone far before I had my little sack of parched coffee out, and was chewing and eating the grains. To my great comfort, I had very little headache that day. If I had been older, I should have been perhaps a little more public in the use of the coffee I carried with me, and have troubled the families to prepare it; yet I could not find it in my heart, young and inexperienced as I was, to reflect on the diet they gave me, by saying, in presenting another article, that they might have had better. I made it a rule to partake of what they gave me, and "ask no questions for conscience' sake," nor did I ever ask for more. My own way of curing a "thorn in my flesh" I kept to myself. As to the mere luxury of eating, I cared less for it than at any period of my life. I only wanted enough, and it of a kind that would make me feel well; for my "meat and drink" was to do the will of Him who had called me, and enrolled me in the high office of the ministry.

Meeting with an Old Greek Grammar.

I found in making the first round—in which I had to survey out the country with my own eyes, and learn all of it I could from the people, in order to as complete an organization as possible—that I had but little time for reading, and for studying the books that belonged to the first year's course of study. I, therefore, was inclined to postpone this matter for awhile. It was, however, on this first round that I resolved on the study of the Greek language. I had in my school-days, as you are aware, given little attention to any other than the English language. I had some knowledge of the Latin, to be sure—at least enough to very cleverly take up the Greek. That which inspired me to the Greek is the importance of that language to the preacher; but that which inspired me to commence the study of that language under circumstances so peculiar, and at a time so unexpected, was the accidental discovery of an old Greek grammar, which was nearly whole. It looked a little like it had straggled away from its proper country, but I thought it had as well be put to use. I got permission to drop it into my circuit treasury department; yet it looked a little oldish—bore a rather strange contrast as it lay by my coffee-sack, which but recently had found its own lodgment. This old book and my Bible were my constant companions in my first six weeks' campaign; but before I had returned to the village from which I started, I found I was striking *tupto* as best I could; but I found that *tupto struck* in so many moods and tenses, and in so many unlooked-for ways, that the battle became pretty hot between us; but I determined on the victory, and obtained it.

DESCRIPTIONS—MASTER PAYTON.

It was about three weeks after I started, when I found myself at a beautiful mountain peak. This was a beautiful section of country on the western slope of the upper cross woods, having a surface gradually undulating. Here and there the higher grounds were overtopped with trees, either standing alone or in beautiful mats. But that which gave grandeur to the place, and which was the principal object of interest to the traveler, was the mountain peak, which rises so abruptly from the plain, and to such a height, that it gave much fatigue to reach the summit.

Here I found seven families, all of whom depended on their herds for a living. This was the very border of the frontier. Here I found a stockade into which they could retreat in case of "Indian troubles," as they called it. I organized these people into a class, or congregation, and preached to them before I left. The people were less restive out here about the Indians than thirty or forty miles farther in. They called this the frontier, and farther in "the settlements;" yet many of those still more remote from this point regarded themselves on the frontier, for the reason that the Indians depredated in their sections, though far east of the extreme border.

The policy of the Indians, in the main, was not to molest the people living on the extreme border, for several reasons. They did not care to steal their cattle, because they had plenty of buffalo and other wild game, which they preferred and regarded more savory as a diet. They did not regard the cow-ponies as a very valuable stock, and this was the general character of the horse property on the border. Again, they loved to keep the peace of the border people, and cultivated it with the view that they would be less diligent in watching, and therefore, with this advantage, that they themselves could make inroads far into the settlements and bring out horses far more valuable than the cow-ponies along the border.

I shall call attention to one family with whom I staid a night and part of a day. They very well illustrate the border people, with whom the rules of society and of family government are not very restraining. This family was as kind as any one need want to be with, yet they had a very careless manner of entertaining strangers. The traveler was regarded as capable of taking care of himself, and therefore they put themselves to little trouble to watch over him or attend to his wants. They made no bills against the general traveler, but parted with him by saying, "Call again." The stranger or traveler among them was at liberty at any time to converse with them, or if he chose, read, study, sit, stand, walk, or do any other reputable business, without the respect generally paid to the rules of decorum. With this family any thing was in order that the whim of any mind might set a-going; and yet it was very seldom that they all accorded into one mind. They presented very much the appearance of a variant buzz—each one for himself. They appeared to be born unto variety. In each one, large and small, existed and dwelt a natural independency of volition as a kind of spontaneous production ingrafted in his nature by the freedom of the air he breathed. Toward the going down of the sun you might see three or four boys, from ten to thirteen years of age, romping and practicing with their lariats, looped in lasso fashion, either catching one another as they ran by or practicing on the calves in the pen. You might see a cow-boy or two, apparently in lonely mood, singing some nonsensical ditty or love song, with a flippant motion of the head and reeling motion of body. Some one calling for one thing, another ordering something else, interluded with the screams of a girl or two at the cow-pen, who, however, can never make any one understand what they want. The bleating of calves and lowing of cattle give a climax to the close of day that chime in equally musical with all the rest. This is a faint picture, but will suffice in some degree to give an idea of the noise, bustle, and confusion that closes the day in the family of a stock-raising man in the West, where there is little regard had for family government. On the frontier, where people depend on their herds, and do not cultivate the soil, there is never much restraint exercised by parents over their children, or over those whom they employ.

I made it a custom to talk with the children wherever I met with them. I naturally have an aptness in this way, and have seldom met with any whom I could not enlist. I never began with them too soberly, and with reproofs. I found it very convenient to begin with schools and education. Nearly all boys feel an interest in these things, and will talk on these subjects readily. Several boys entered the room at one time, where I was engaged in reading, and appeared disposed to be still. I soon engaged them in conversation. I asked them if they had a school in their neighborhood. They answered in the negative. I asked them if they could read and write. They answered again in the negative. One of them, about eleven years of age, and who led the others, said: "I can spell though." I let out to him several words of several syllables each, but to every one he shook his head. There was a little pause in our conversation, when he looked up inquiringly at me and asked why I did not give him "*baker.*" "Ah! well," said I, "then spell baker;" for I saw that first word of a child's ambition, who is taught in Webster, was held fondly in his memory. He spelled it after the fashion of a half-taught child, unfortunately prolonging the *key-r-ker* on the last syllable. Our conversation here ended on day-schools and general education.

My next step was to lead out on Sunday-schools. Said I, "Have you ever had a Sunday-school in this settlement?" "A Sunday-school!" wonderingly said the talkative little Payton; "what is that?" I explained how the people met with their children on Sunday, read the Bible and asked questions about it, continuing my remarks to some length; to all of which Payton said: "We do n't have no such thing as that here. We rest on Sundays, though we work sometimes; but *pap* says he would like to quit it, though he do n't know how he can, as long as he has got all these cattle. But I know he would not send us to such a school as that, for we have got more to do now on Sundays than he wants us to do." I saw at once that this lad had a very faint idea of what is meant by a Sunday-school. He looked upon it as much a perversion of the Sabbath as hunting, marking, and branding cattle. He estimated it as work, and therefore a desecration of the day, on that account.

I now led off in a catechising lecture, in which I assumed how the power of God was displayed in the creation; how he formed the earth. I was going to say more, but the keen-witted and quick-speaking Payton interrupted me before I had finished. He had been used to putting in a word whenever he chose, and of excepting to any thing he disliked. Said he, "Did you say that one man made this world?" alluding, as I perceived, to the earth. "No, Payton," I said; "God made the world." "Well," said he, "ain't he just one?" "Yes, Payton," said I; "he is one, but he is not a man." To this the marvelous little Payton replied that "no one man and no one any thing else made the world. All the men in this country could n't make the mountain peak, standing out yonder." Just then, I heard one of them in a drawling tone say: "No, they could n't, for it's too big."

I saw at once that little Payton had the victory, according to the judges, who had been attentively listening. I had to give it up. I had more than my match. The yoke these lads put upon my neck was galling me. The want of more definite ideas of God and the skepticism that had crept into their young minds were evidently the fruits of parental neglect. O that parents could realize the great importance of properly instructing and training their children! It is a business far more important than rearing herds and building barns. What a charge will come against some of them in the great day for neglecting to teach their children in the paths in which they should walk!

No one is satisfied with defeat. I felt a determination to try and regain some of my lost honors. I wanted to get even with this little imp of a skeptic. He had routed me on two fields. Said I, "Payton, what do you do of Sundays?" "We do n't do much of any thing now," said he, "but when it's warm weather, we brand the calves and yearlings till dinner that the boys have been hunting through the week." Here he stopped. "But, Payton," said I, "what do you do after dinner?" "Well," said he, "you see, pap and the boys are tired, and they leave it to me and Bill and Tom to drive the cattle *outen* the pens. If you ever seen fun, then we have it. You see, when we pull down the bars, we fix some rails and things so the cattle can't see us; then I'll lay down under the bars and things with a sharp stick, and then tell Bill and Tom to drive one at a time, and just as he jumps over, I stick him under, and he says *ba;* and they keep driving until I miss one, then it's Bill's time; and when he misses one, then it's Tom's time; but I always make more of them say *ba* than Bill and Tom both." I had but one more feeble shaft. I concluded to let it fly and quit the field. Said I, "Payton, how can you tell when you make a miss?" "Why, you see," said he, "we always count it a miss when she don't say *ba*." What he meant by *she* was one of the cattle.

I concluded to have no more talk with the boys while I remained in the vicinity of the mountain peak, and more especially with the remarkable Payton, whose history, if it were known up to the present time, would in all probability lay the foundation for an attractive romance. I have often wished that I had a picture of that remarkable and peculiar boy; not, however, for my own enjoyment, for he stereotyped his image on my memory, but that I might show it to others; but whatever enjoyment there may be in it to others is lost, for being no painter myself I cannot copy it. Now, dear mother, I hope you will by no means think that I am trying to make a hero of the inimitable little Payton. I saw your occasional smiles under the narration, yet, believe me, I have the same virtuous lips with which you launched me out on manhood's stage.

I left the vicinity of this mountain peak, to be back again in six weeks. I felt resolved to try another battle with Payton on my return. You know, you raised me with pluck to the bone, and never to quit my foe as long as I was the under dog. But this one I never met again, and probably well enough too, for such a frontier boy as Payton is as unabating in true courage as load-stone is in attraction, and neither will ever let steel alone. But I never saw this young hero again, yet I visited the vicinity of the mountain peak regularly every six weeks during the year. This hero of a boy, though, was always out after cattle or on some other mission; but wherever he was, I have no doubt that he was making history.

PREACHING IN A FRONTIER DWELLING-HOUSE—HOW THE PEOPLE GO TO PREACHING ON THE FRONTIER.

I, having opportunity, had sent forward an appointment to the head-waters of a creek, away to the south-west of the county-town that had but recently been located and laid off. I had only a pleasant jaunt of twelve or thirteen miles on the morning of the appointment. It was, however, mostly a pathway through the woods, and I had never traveled it before. However, at eleven o'clock, I found myself at a Mr. Hamilton's, the place appointed for the service. The man by whom I sent the appointment met me and conducted me into a genuine model of a frontier preaching-place—a private dwelling—one room, and that's all. Upon a bedpost hung half a dozen or more six-shooters.. Several guns were sitting up in the corners of the house, and a few were leaning against the wall on the outside. Two or three of the congregation sat in a leaning-forward posture, with their guns resting against their shoulders, and muzzles up. The house being small was of course crowded with the people, and other things it contained. Notwithstanding this, occasionally a dog might be seen twisting and fairly pushing himself through the crowd, now and then looking up into the faces of the people, until at last he found his master, when, as if satisfied, with a wag of his tail, and after a look of complacency, he would retreat to the door again. The table was out-doors under a brush arbor, as well as all culinary things. The benches were of split logs, mounted on legs, or of any other sort of thing convenient, for the people appeared by no means hard to please.

When these people, and others similarly situated, went to church, they left no one behind. If it were a day free from Indian alarm, the preacher might always count on a good congregation, if there were enough people in the settlement to make one, for men, women, and children all go. They go not only for the novelty of preaching, which they but seldom get, but for safety. The dogs go, nor do the cats stay away, and in a few instances I have known some chickens to follow. There is a kind feeling of fellowship subsisting between all the partners of a frontier residence.

Leave Hamilton's for the West Fork of the Trinity River—Luck of the Night.

After preaching, I started about three o'clock for a settlement on the West Fork of the Trinity, a distance of thirty miles. I would like to have staid longer with the people here, but my object was to reach another county-seat by the approaching Sunday, in which I had a preärrangement to preach on that day. Therefore I had to be frugal of daylight, lest I should not be able to organize the missions up to that place by that time.

There was no direct road in the direction I wanted to go. My route was along a few paths through rather open woods, but more frequently without any beaten track at all. It was reported to me that a few scattering settlers lay in my way, but that it would be rather accidental to find one of them, and therefore get a night's lodging. Some even forewarned me that if I did not take care I would get caught out for the night. But, as I thought, being a pretty fair hand to keep a course, I did not feel specially uneasy, and therefore a little carelessly launched out on my course. I believed fully in a superintending Providence, and that it was my duty to go. I believed it would all work well enough for the night. I set out under the best instructions I could get, determined to follow, as nearly as I could the direction given. It was the most plenteous region for wild-turkeys I ever saw. Close pistol-shot to them was not at all difficult, they were so indifferent to the presence of a human being. I think their range had been little interrupted for many years. I would have fired on them, but it appeared foolish to kill innocent creatures for which I had no use. Again, I scarcely knew where I was, nor in what proximity to me there lurked a secret foe. I thought it prudent, therefore, and preferred to ride on in silence through a pathless woodland.

Toward night-fall, a semi-weary anxiety came over me in reference to the night. I was anxious to find some trace of civilization, for I had seen none since I had been on this lonely route. If I could only have seen where the recent strokes of the settler's ax had chipped a tree, where wagon-wheels had impressed the ground, or in the distance heard the low of an ox, or the neigh of a horse, it would have brought relief to my suspense. The sun was just sinking to rest when, to my surprise and pleasure, I came unexpectedly and suddenly upon a habitation with no fenced field. A small house with one room and a moderate yard-fence, and that's all.

Said I to the lord of this independency, "How do you do, sir?" "Moderate," said he; "what of yourself?" "Very well," said I, "except I hardly know where I am. I would like to get lodging with you for the night; can you take me in?" "Well, yes, if you can put up with our way of living." "I can certainly do that, sir," said I, "and thank you." I alighted and tied my horse, or in Western phraseology "staked" him, on the best mat of grass around. My host was a little busy with some evening business, until the deep duskiness of the evening had gathered around, at which time supper was served; after which, while his wife was cleaning away the things, and putting their two little children to bed, he engaged me in conversation. He seemed anxious to find out something of me and my business. Perhaps, if my voice had been toned up unnaturally, after the manner of a benediction, like some preachers with whom I have met, he would readily have known both me and my business; but my tone of voice then, as now you find it is, was just such as is common with my fellow-men. It had no long-noted humdrum, no deep, grave-yard hollowness. I could never see why the tone of a man's voice should change, though he become President of the United States. But let us not run off on too many tangent lines of thought—let us come again to our narrative.

Said my host: "Are you a surveyor, sir, locating lands?" "No, sir," said I; "yet I understand that science, having studied both Davie and Gummere." This latter statement I made because I thought it would be pleasant enough to talk on that subject. "I thought," said he, "you might have a compass in your saddle-bags." After a pause, said he, "Are you looking out for a stock-ranch?" "No," said I, "I am not looking for a ranch, though I own a few horses in this State." "Where is your ranch?" said he. To this I gave a direct answer. "How long have you been in Texas?" said he. I told him three years. Said he: "Have you got land certificates, and looking for a place to locate them?" Said I: "No; I once speculated in them and got badly served on account of so many of them being a fraud. I think I will never have any thing more to do with land certificates." "I suppose," said he, "you have some relations along on the frontier, and you have come out to see them?" "No, sir," said I, "my relations are generally in Kentucky; some in Missouri, and a few in Oregon." "What is your name?" said he. I told him, yet he appeared as ignorant as ever of my mission. I do not believe he would have guessed it in a week. He looked wonderingly and confused, and had but little more to say. I knew he was soliloquizing in his mind, and was anxious to know something more definite of the stranger whom he had taken in. Said I: "My friend, I will tell you who I am and what my business is." He and his wife were all attention immediately.

"I am," said I, "a Methodist circuit-rider, to organize the people into congregations, and to preach to them the gospel. My business is to go all up and down the border of the settlements from Red River a hundred miles south." He looked at his wife and then looked at me, then looking wonderingly away, he faintly murmured, "A preacher." I am satisfied he never saw a preacher before, on the border. He was secluded from the settlements, and perhaps had not heard of a preacher since he had settled that place.

By and by he casually observed that he thought it bed-time. I remarked that I was always governed by the taste of the family with which I stopped. As often as two or three times he called my attention to the fact that it was growing late. I thought I discovered what was his trouble. Owing to certain training they have received, there are people who think it respectful to have prayers in their family, when a preacher visits them, yet they know not how to introduce the matter, and wait for him; and I suppose if he does not take a hint, or have courage, or stands back stiffly on the rules of etiquette, where there is none and where it should not be expected, he will be in danger sometimes of sitting up all night. There are a few preachers who need to be served just that way; for they get a part of their education by thumps and kicks; and then sometimes they call it abuse, turn sour, make faces, and get angry, because the whole world, with one-tenth the opportunity, is not as well cultivated as they imagine themselves.

With this philosophical view of the subject, I lifted my friend out of his entanglement, for I plainly saw he was of opinion that the preacher should manage prayers in the family the same as any other service. Therefore said I: "It is the custom of us Methodist preachers to have prayers in the families with which we stop. If you approve it, we will have prayers before we retire." "Certainly, certainly," said he. Then looking toward his wife, he said: "Mary, fix a light." Then to me he said: "Have you a book? We had one, but somehow it got scattered while we were coming out here." I told him that I had a "book"—that is, the Bible—but at the same time discovered that his wife was considerably flurried over getting a light. The oil she used at supper flickered and waned, and I was satisfied she had none to replenish with. I thought I would relieve her, and remarked that we would dispense with reading. "We will, however," said I, "sing a familiar hymn and then pray." I began a hymn which I thought everybody knew, and I thought they could easily chime in with me. It was "Soldier of the Cross." When I began to sing, two large, ferocious dogs, which had up to that time been quiet, began to chime in with me, instead of the man and woman. It was not the lamenting howl they often give to a sounding horn, but an angry, vicious, spiteful bark. Yet I sung on, and they barked on. The only difference was that while the circumstances had a tendency to keep me cooled down in tone, their vicious loudness increased continually. The hills and woods began to echo back dismally. But by and by the song was finished, and as I hoped the barking too. But no; for when we got down to prayers, the man at one end of their small house, the wife at the other, and I between them near the door-way, which was open, the noise of the barking still continued. Though I was not boisterous in my prayer, nor peculiarly solemn, yet the dogs barked more fiercely than before. They now began to run as they barked. They could not understand what was going on, and being dogs, they acted their part well by keeping up a racket that would frighten away demons, if such a thing could be done by noise. But at last they found the varmint. They came to the door, and as vociferously barked at me as if I had been a panther. I prayed on, but that injunction "Watch" was literally and practically obeyed. One of the dogs in his eager spirit jumped half in at the door and snapped at me as though he would tear me. I gave way a little from the door and the dog, but had not yet concluded. The good wife could stand it no longer. She was up, and with a stick, just as he came at me again, struck him across the back and sent him howling away; at the same time she called out in earnest tones, "Joseph, get a board!" "Amen!" said I; and in a little quicker time than it is usually done, we were all on our feet and ready for the foe.

This incident, at the time it happened, did not appear at all amusing to me, but I never narrated it to a friend unless I could see his lips curl with humor. If I had been older and more experienced in the ministry, I should in all probability have taken in the situation to better advantage. I might have stopped until quiet was restored; but like many a young preacher, I knew no stopping-place until I had made my full round of prayer. I trained myself afterward to stop anywhere and to begin anywhere, according to the circumstances. As it relates to this good man and his wife, I have always thanked them in my heart. They took me in at night-fall when I was lost, and in a wild, desolate place. They gave me of the best diet they had, and a pillow for my weary head. They willingly and cheerfully treated me kindly, though perhaps I was a burden to them. They shall be remembered by me kindly as long as I remember the incident that occurred the night I staid with them. The prayer of that night was not the last I have offered for that family. What became of them I know not; but often and often my soul has breathed out for the man, his wife, and the two darling little children. The next morning, a little after the rising of the sun, I left them, advising them to seek the settlements, not thinking, however, what would have become of me that night had they not settled at that place. It is an unnatural act for a man to settle as that one did in a wild country remote from the settlements. However it may be I know not, but this I do know, that God provided in this way for one of his weary pilgrims. How many more have been similarly provided for I shall never know.

The Evil of Dancing.

I found my way through to the west fork of the Trinity whither I had started, organized a class, or rather a congregation, and then met my Sabbath appointment. I saw the intensest excitement prevailed in the town. A party had fled away who had shot two men through, and could not be found. An old man was accused of harboring him, and the street talk was almost as severe against the old man as against the culprit. I was afraid they would visit the death penalty on the old man for his reported obliquity. I inquired into the nature of the affair, learned that they had a dancing party in town, and that the affair took place in the ball-room. My congregation was small considering the place, owing to the intense excitement that prevailed.

How strange it is that so many people indorse the ball-room, and dancing, when it is such a fruitful source, such a prolific stem of so much hate, sorrow, and crime! Just to think of the unrest of that young culprit for his rash act; of the sorrow that brooded in the hearts of his once doting father and his loving mother; of the excitement it occasioned throughout the whole town and over a large section of the country; of the abuse heaped upon the old man for alleged assistance to the guilty, and of the old man's narrow escape from an excited and enraged mob; of the suffering, bleeding, dying young men, the victims of the night; of the sorrow of fathers, mothers, brothers, and sisters, as they hear their dying-groans—just to think of these as only a part of the fruits of the evil of dancing, and it is enough to chill the blood with horror, and be a standing argument along-side the verdict of the best society of the land that the ball-room is a great moral evil, and the fruitful source of varied crimes. Its evils are not confined to a single sex. It is the dark sneak that legalizes a liberty between the sexes that would be frowned down and execrated under any other circumstances, and in this way leads to the perversion of the soul and the debasement of character.

I was riding along one day, and my attention was called to some men digging by the road-side. I stopped and asked them what they were doing. They, pointing to a house on a hill not far off, said: "There was a dance up there last night; a man was killed, and we are fixing to bury him."

I once saw an old man, accompanied by a lawyer, traveling to a distant town to see his son there lodged in jail. The old man appeared in deep sorrow. I learned from the lawyer that the old man's son had shot two men in an affray growing out of the troubles of a dancing-party.

I lodged for the night once in a community where the nerves of the people were shocked over a tragedy which had just occurred in their midst. I asked for its history. An old Christian lady answered as follows: "For many years our community was one of the most peaceful. We had no neighborhood quarrels; no neighbor entered a lawsuit against another; the young people all loved one another. But about two years ago, some of the young people thought they must have a dance. We let them have their way. They have been keeping it up ever since. I see now there has been more unfriendly feeling and hate these two years than ever before. The dance has been the source of discord. No man ever got drunk in our community until about a year ago. But night before last, Joe Wilson, as good a young man as we had among us, was stabbed to death at the dance."

There may be what are called fashionable *balls*, but they are without piety. Arguments may be made that the ball-room, or dance, is necessary to improve the manners, but those who can learn good manners only in this way are certainly the stupidest of all the nation. Men may say in admiration, "That lady waltzes gracefully," but it is at the expense of her virtue. Mothers may boast of this accomplishment among their daughters, but it does not spring from a broad brain. The practice of Washington City may be pleaded in vindication of dancing, yet this city may be as foul in Heaven's view as any in America. Hundreds gather there seeking victims. It is useless to vindicate the ball-room. Its history is a rebuking comment to such a disciple. It brings up in gloomy array the smoldering virtue of too many thousands who have gone down under its perverting influences. If the young men of the nation would turn State's evidence in the case, there is not a virtuous cheek in all the land that would not blush at the rehearsal. It would be such an *exposé* as would open the eyes of many to see how ruinous is this popular and enchanting evil. But we must stop. May God in his goodness speedily work a moral revolution in the minds of the people that will sound the death-knell to the ball-room, which is a kind of head-quarters in the business, and therefore unpopularize dancing all over the land.

Snuffing the War-breeze.

I now left this place for the extreme southern limit of the mission work. Here was the best improvement I had seen. It was entirely free from Indian excitement. Political partyism, however, was most exciting. Mr. Lincoln was soon to be sworn President of the United States; some States had seceded. Texas was getting all ablaze with excitement. The lower part of the mission work had caught the political distemper, and declared its readiness to bear its part in the coming conflict. The people were talking war. They regarded that a party was going into power whose creed, when thoroughly sifted and understood, was violative of the Constitution of the

United States, and meant, in one form or another, war upon existing slavery unto its speedy and ultimate overthrow. They regarded that the "irrepressible conflict" had come; that the issue was at their doors; that they had to meet it; that they had warded it off as long as they could. The war-god was in the air. The nation's nostrils were full of his foul exhalations. It is true I was a Democrat. I was always a Southerner in feeling and sympathy. But opening Pandora's box just at this time—just as I was learning how to preach, just as I had entered out on my first work, just when I felt no zeal for using carnal weapons—was most harassing to me. The people's minds seemed to have taken a tangent from religion. When I would talk of Christ, the people would talk of Mr. Lincoln. When I would talk of the doctrine of the New Testament, they would talk of the doctrine of political parties. When I went home with them, they could not remember the text, yet they could repeat whole columns of news from the papers. All this was indeed distressing to the young preacher, yet he had it to endure. He resolved to go on, however, regardless of politics or war, and to organize, preach, talk to the children, visit, study, and do all the work of a pastor as best he knew how. Every thing indicated a general spiritual decline. I knew it would take hard work, and constant work, to keep the people's minds on Christ.

Meeting with Universalism.

On this part of the work I met with several Universalists, who, as I had been informed, were in the habit of showing the preachers no quarters. Contact with them corroborated what had come to my ears. There was no use in trying to evade them— one of them especially. He regarded himself as the man of the country. He seemed not to care for the political stew in which the country was involved. He was a monomaniac, and universal salvation of the souls of men as a finality was his theme. He was more ostentatious than wise. He found where I was going, and therefore hunted me down for a victim. There are men in the world who will sacrifice time and means, or, as it is stated in the Holy Word, "will compass sea and land, to make one proselyte; and when he is made, he is threefold more the child of the devil than before." Fortunately, I had seen and heard much of Universalism. It was by no means new or strange to me. It was by no means a shock to my nerves to meet with this stalwart man of his class. Said I, "My friend, do you understand Greek?" for I had my old Greek grammar in my hand which I had found on the mission work about sixty miles away. "O yes," said he, with, as I thought, a pressed air of complacency. I then struck out on *tupto* with manifest familiarity, and asked him to conjugate it in the second aorist. "Ah!" said he, "I don't care to do that." "Ah!" said I, "you must do it, or else I will not pick up the gauntlet you are in a habit of staving around so fearlessly." I could not prevail on him to try his hand in Greek grammar, and for a very good reason: he knew as little of Greek as I did, but at the time he thought he knew far less. Said I again: "My friend, do you not intend, in the event we have a discussion, to refer to Greek etymology for proofs of what you may assert to be the true meaning of words?" To this he gave an answer so evasive and vague as to impress me that he knew not one word of Greek, lest it be *aionias*, the favorite and general text of Universalists. Yet he credited me with a far better knowledge of the language than I possessed. In this, I considered that I had a decided advantage. Nor did he, according to his custom, upbraid me for superstition and ignorance. "Now," said I, "my friend, I am going to lay before you certain principles of doctrine which I regard as axiomatically true, and I shall never have any thing to say to you on your doctrine until you disprove them. I think you will sweat over them more than Hercules did in cleaning the stables of King Augeus. Yet, Hercules was a wonderful worker; for he is credited with cleaning the stables in a single day, where three thousand oxen had been fed for thirty years. You shall have a Herculean task, and you will have to go at it in a Herculean way. These principles I hold to be true:

"1. The first attribute of the Deity revealed is power. This is revealed in the creation.

"2. The second attribute revealed of Deity is justice. This is seen in the penalty of death visited for touching and eating the interdicted fruit.

"3. The attribute of love, and consequent mercy

growing out of it, is third in the order of its manifestation to the world. This is seen in the promise alluding to the seed of the woman, or Christ: 'It shall bruise thy head.'

"4. No attribute in the divine character can be abused through the influence of any other attribute.

"5. Man, by creation being a free moral agent, was provided with only a conditional salvation. In it, justice holds over the penalty, awaiting results.

"6. Man originally had the capacity to keep the law, and therefore glorify God with perfect obedience.

"7. Under the promise and gift of God, man has now by grace a parallel capacity.

"8. If one sin of original transgression merited eternal punishment, and the escape was only provided for through intercession, it will certainly fall no less severely on all free agents for whom escape was made, if they do not comply with the conditions.

"9. A man is not saved or lost primarily by the law, but by the divine character. The law which is revealed, and which affixes the penalty, is but the outcropping of the true divine character, which is both stern and immutable.

"10. There are some created intelligences in the universe who are now moral wrecks, without hope or any system of relief, and who are now separated from the better class of their kind who kept their first estate.

"11. There are impossibilities, mathematical, physical, and moral, with God. He cannot make three and two less nor more than five; nor one part of a circle more remote than another part from the center. He cannot make a thing be and not be at the same time, nor a stick with just one end. God is not absurd. He cannot be God and forgive the impenitent, save a sinner in heaven, nor send a Christian to hell.

"12. A man dies a Christian or a sinner, and thereby seals his relation for eternity.

"13. So far as we can learn from His word, he has but two places for angels and men—heaven and hell. The process of Universalists in destroying the one by any arguments on definitive words annihilates the other.

"Now, sir," said I, "these are principles which I hold to, and they are true. You cannot refute them, and you need not try. They are enough to give any Universalist in America the lock-jaw. Until you take them up one at a time and disprove their truth, I shall have nothing more to say to you on doctrine." I acknowledge that it did not logically follow that my opponent was put to the necessity and hard task of proving a negative; nevertheless, this was the way of it, and it was effectual enough for the time.

There are people in the world more valuable than wise. This was one of them. He had infested that settlement in a mouthing way long enough; and long enough had been diffusing his poison and making minced-meat of the weak and ignorant. But now, like a tail-picked peacock, he was completely settled. He never rallied under the turn I made to beat him by laying down principles of doctrnne. What became of him I know not. The last I knew of him he was known under the name of "Old Lock-jaw."

The Recount.

I was not much longer in completing my first campaign and in organizing the missions so far as it was devolved on myself, and soon found myself again where I began my mission work—the place where I was once tempted to desert the ministry, and in which I could again see my young friend "Jesse," and hear him sing. I had seen no Indians, and so far as I knew had made no hair-breadth escapes. I had been continually going for nearly six weeks; the organization was about complete. I had now preached nineteen times; at a few places I preached twice. I had for my next campaign a list of twenty-three appointments, with a probable increase of them. I had been closely occupied, but did not feel weary—could preach pretty much to my satisfaction now, though, of course, it was but poor preaching at best.

Now, dear mother, I have narrated to you one campaign on the missions. They were repeated regularly every six weeks until the close of the Conference-year. I have given you the first, as the most important one, somewhat in detail. To give them all in detail, as each succeeded the other, would, in many respects, be monotonous. I will not weary you with such a course, but will lead on in a way that shows variety, which, you know, is the spice of things. I think I know the kind of *bouquet* you used to love, and from that memory I shall try and make the arrangement that will please you well. I will close my work on the missions with sketches, reminiscences, and anecdotes, which I know you love so well. Such a taste and love I have inherited from you. Never have I grown weary when hearing a good narrator tell of these; and the book that contains them is always full of interest to me. Now, to begin, I invite you to

An Old Lady who Had Seen Better Days.

While making the campaigns of the missions, I scarcely ever got into that vicinity without stopping with a certain good man at least for a dinner, if not for a night. This good brother was a preacher, grown somewhat old; was a little lame, slow of speech, but greatly respected and loved by all the people. I saw in his house, among the other members of his family, an old lady of singular costume and habits. Her reason was much wasted, and her articulation very indistinct, which, as I afterward learned, was brought on her by disease. From the first time I saw this sad spectacle in the form of a human being, she often occupied my thoughts when at other points, and surrounded by very different circumstances; for there was an outline developed in her manner, and a background in her countenance that indicated she once had better days, and was deserving of a better fate. It was an outline, though stained, which neither time nor misfortune could wash away. I did, somewhere in my *diary*, note the name of this interesting and unfortunate lady, but the leaf has been lost. It was not until in the summer season following my first sight of her that I learned a sketch of her history. It was accidental. The good man, of whom I have already spoken, invited me to a seat on the porch as the pleasantest for a hot summer day. When I entered the porch, there I saw this object of my sketch lying on a comfortable-looking pallet, apparently indifferent to all that was going on around. In some way I scarcely hold in memory now, the names of Washington and Jefferson were called. Thereupon, suddenly, as if aroused by some unexpected shock, the emaciated and pitiable old lady on the pallet, who had noticed nothing before, aroused as from sleep, raised herself on her elbows, and with eyes enlivened, in her indistinct utterance called the names of Washington, Jefferson, Adams, and others who were distinguished men at the nation's capital in the latter part of the eighteenth and in the beginning of the nineteenth century. She appeared, in her incoherent manner, anxious to converse with me of those men, and of those times. In her feeble and semi-demented manner, I could see more distinctly the traces of a high culture that made her in her girlhood days the associate and guest of the best society at the capital of the country.

I could not learn the full history of this unfortunate lady. Her page had been a blank sheet for a long time. Adversity in young womanhood had turned on her his grinding heel. In wrestling with poverty, she had gradually sunken down into comparative obscurity, making her page for many years a blank sheet on which no one troubled himself to write, and whose bright surface had been abused only by the lapse of time and the tears of sorrow which she shed. When I looked on this sad relic of humanity and learned something of her history, it sent a pain to my heart. Alas! thought I, how varied is human life here below! What lonely hills we sometimes climb! What beautiful things, in enraptured vision, we sometimes behold from their summits! Yet how often, before the round of life is made, force of circumstances drives us down on the other side among the groveling things in the valley below!

Isaiah xxviii. 20.

"The bed is shorter than that a man can stretch himself on it; and the covering narrower than that he can wrap himself in it." To be compelled to go to bed on such a bed and with such cover, in the time of a blue Texas Norther, was enough to make me wish that such a custom as going to bed and sleeping had never been invented. Why, what can a man do in such a fix? He can't lie down gracefully; he can't cover himself decently; but—he can *shiver*. Well, that is doing something, to be sure; but it is the thing he does n't want to do, and yet the very thing he cannot help doing. Such is some of our experience on the missions. On such occasions I never felt like studying Greek, of conjugating the verb *tupto*, nor of trying to recall any of the words of that language. I would not, under the circumstances, have discussed the question of religion with a Universalist. I did not even feel like spending my time in prayer; nor did I feel like calling for more cover or a larger bed—for I knew the good people did for me the best they could. It is only a little of the sacrifice a man must bear who is called to preach the gospel and goes—anywhere. Well, I will tell you how I learned to do before I shivered many nights. I learned not to go to bed at all—that is, in the ordinary way of stripping off to the freezing point; yet there are some men who have such a liking for this custom, and it exerts such imperial sway over them, that they follow it against reason, common sense, comfort, and every thing else that might be named. Well, let them go on—shiver—freeze; I have no objection. But I will do again, under the circumstances, just as I did then—just the reverse. Instead of stripping, I would go down into my treasury department and find more clothes, and put them on too. I would just not go to bed at all. I would just lie down as I ride a horse, overcoat and all, only minus spurs and boots. If the bed was too short, I contracted. If the cover was to narrow, I wrapped it around my feet. If I wanted to turn over, I wouldn't do it. If I got in pain, I learned to endure. If I thought I could stand it no longer, I knew I could. I knew I had to be still; for I learned from experience the irreparable damage inflicted by tossing about when lying down cold. Just move once, and then shiver the remainder of the night. If one is up in the cold, let him take exercise to keep warm; but if he is lying down in the cold, let him keep still if he wants not to freeze. I will not grow solemn over the matter, but I must say, though I have not done it latterly, and never in the public congregation nor around the family altar, yet I have many a time prayed: "Good Lord, deliver me from such a bed as Isaiah describes when he says, 'The bed is shorter than that a man can stretch himself on it; and the covering narrower than that he can wrap himself in it.'"

THE UNLUCKY NIGHT.

It had been a beautiful day, followed by a beautiful night, that I retired to rest toward the north-west border of the mission work. When I retired, I felt a calm satisfaction creep over me. My mood of mind and heart readily enticed the folding arms of Morpheus, and soon I had lost sight of all surrounding things, and "nature's sweet restorer" was preparing me for the arduous labors of another day. It was near to the hour of midnight, when "deep sleep falls on man," or about the time of night the Greeks left Tenedos for Troy, that I heard the low and rather solemn call of my name. I faintly heard at first, then more distinctly, and finally aroused and looked. The gentleman of the house was up, dressed, gun in hand and six-shooter buckled around him. His sixteen-year-old son was armed, and stood with the utmost composure. The wife stood around with a half-afraid, anxious look. There was talking going on among them in a low tone. I comprehended immediately that they had evidences that the Indians were in the settlement. Soon being armed, with six-shooter in hand, said I: "My friend, what evidences have you that the Indians are in the country?" Said he: "The very best, and I fear the family over the way have been murdered." This announcement made me feel very sad. Whereupon I asked him for the evidences in the case. He continued by saying that he never heard such screaming as he heard over there awhile ago; that evidently something was up. I listened, but could hear nothing. Said I: "My friend, I will tell you what we will do. You stay here, and I and James will go and reconnoiter the place and find out what is done." Against this course the wife most solemnly protested, and in the wildest manner insisted that if their house were attacked all of us would be necessary to make a defense. Thereupon my friend and brother remarked that "what was done over there could not be helped or mended now." I said no more. After a little while, he remarked that he was afraid the Indians would get his horses. This reminded me that my faithful George was as much exposed. Said I: "Can we not guard our horses with safety to your family?" "Yes," said he, "if we guard our horses we can save them; and if the Indians make an attack on the house, a few shots into them from the outside will put them in confusion and drive them into hasty retreat."

Accordingly, we guarded our horses in a lot near by until the dawning of the day. The night had passed away in the utmost stillness, except the barking of dogs throughout the night, which betokened to frontiersmen that all was not right. Now said my friend: "I will step over yonder where I heard the screaming of the women, and you and James can stay here awhile yet." He went, and soon returned. There was a humorous and pleasant grin on his face, and just as much of it as could be expected after losing a night's rest, and harassed with suspense and anxiety. "My brother," said I, "let us hear your report." "There is nobody killed or scalped," said he, with the grin on his face now growing broader. "But," said I, "you have kept me up for a night, and I want to know the cause of it." "Well," said he, "about six months ago, the husband of one of the ladies over there went off, and had not been heard of since. About the hour of midnight, last night, he returned." "Is that all?" said I. "That is all," said he. "Is that the cause of all that screaming, by which you thought a whole family was murdered by the Indians?" "That is it," said he. "But come, now," said I, "are there really no Indians in the country?" "None that I have heard of," said he.

I now began to think, without speaking a word of it. I thought of what James said a good while ago: "Behold what a great matter a little fire kindleth." I thought of our suspense and anxiety, of the loss of a good night's rest, and of my own drowsiness. I thought of woman's tongue, and the quick-pulsating chords of the throat; how she can tune these up into an alarming scream on occasions both necessary and unnecessary. I thought, behind all this, of the moving spring to it all—of a delinquent husband, and how much he deserved to be punished. I just thought until I thought myself down, like a hound worn out in the chase, and tried to be content with an affair that was now beyond all amending. But I did resolve never to be troubled, nor to trouble myself, about Indians again, unless I knew they were nearer than forty miles of me.

The Cyclone.

One blustering Sunday, having preached to a respectable congregation, for the West, I went home with a Presbyterian possessed of a large family. He lived in a house built of hewn post-oak logs, with a box-frame, caving to one side, attached. There were two stone chimneys to the north end—one to the frame, and the other to the log part of his dwelling. As the day advanced, the winds began to dash more furiously, as if competing in a race. About three o'clock, a dark, ill-omened cloud appeared a little above the horizon in the north-west, over the face of which, as it grew a little higher, the gulf-clouds moved about as if in sportive play. For awhile this dark-blue cloud seemed to hesitate, and have a doubt whether it would remain back until dissipated into ether-blue or advance and terrify the souls of men. But before five o'clock, all doubt of its intentions had disappeared. It was evidently advancing, and every moment assumed an aspect more threatening. The wind, which before came in fitful gusts, began to drive with a constant pressing force right into the face of the rising monster. It was like two fierce monsters fixing for fierce combat. The driving wind appeared enough to drive back any force;

but that dark-blue monster rather seemed to be hastening to the combat.

Ah! how beautifully grand the sight, and yet accompanied with such awe-inspiring power! Out in the West, on the broad, open prairie, with vision uneclipsed, only on the horizon where the earth and sky meet. Alone? No, not all alone; our trust is in *Him*

> Who plants his footsteps in the sea
> And rules within the storm.

Doors and windows are all securely fastened. I knew not yet what was coming. I had never seen a cyclone. All I knew was that the elements appeared to be tangled and mad. I could hear a roaring like a distant grinding. The wind that for some time had been driving steadily, in the face of the dark, rising cloud, stopped so suddenly that the house fairly cracked on righting itself on relief from the pressure. There is a calm, but the low, growling, grinding sound in rumbling tone is heard near at hand. Up to this time I felt no uneasiness; but something moved me, and without permission I advanced to the door in the west side of the house and opened it, when lo! and not far off, there broke upon my vision a dreadful sky. The cyclone had already burst upon the earth, and here the monster came, dipping from sky to earth, and in revolving tide carrying round and round the clouds and the *débris* of many a ruined thing. I closed the door, and lost no time. "My brother," said I, "quick, quick, a cyclone! If you have a cellar or any under-ground protection, haste into it with your family." He seemed amazed at my action and slow to move. He could not realize, for his eyes had not seen, the dreadful sky. He said there was an under-ground milk-house on the east side of the house. I opened the door and passed out three children who were soon safe in their under-ground retreat. No others would go. Just then—O the indescribable force!—the monster struck the south-west corner of the building. I heard the crash, and thought every thing moved with the driving tide. I sprung immediately from the door in the east toward the subterranean cavity, in which I knew three children were safe. I did not reach it. I was too late. I went a helpless victim along with the rolling tide. I was not conscious of the distance I had been carried, for during this war of elements I found myself thinking of this little milk-house, and clutching to find my way into it. But when I could stand and make my reckoning, I found myself several hundred yards away.

I remember I was in dread of losing my breath through the very force of the winds. I am of opinion some have died in this way. I remember clutching the grass and throwing my face between my arms in order to breathe at all. I had no intention of making observations during this rage of elements, for it was with difficulty that I could see at all; yet occasional glimpses taught me how safe it was to lie low. Every object that had been weighed by the wind was flying with arrow speed. Only ponderous objects came rolling and bounding on the ground. These ordinarily rolling would have a crushing weight, but when almost lifted by the wind were comparatively harmless. Several heavy timbers I saw come bounding toward me. I crouched, felt them push me and then go on their way, doing me no harm.

Now that it was over, I looked around to see how things appeared. Yonder in the distance, I see two stone chimneys standing as high as their shoulders, with a heap of rubbish piled about them. I approach it, passing by the cavern in the ground, when three little heads, peeping out, as if realizing the catastrophe, say, "We are all safe in here." I did not tarry, but remarking, "Remain quiet," hastened into the *débris* of that ruined dwelling. There, crouched under the ruins by one of the chimneys, against which some of the logs had lodged, were the man, his wife, and all the rest of their children, all unhurt, except a slight bruise on the man's head. In a little while, he and I started for the nearest house—his neighbor, a young man that had just brought his bride of Thursday last to his new home. The house was razed to its foundation, but no mortal answered our call. As we pull around in the dark through the rubbish, expecting every moment to find the remains of this newly united and loving pair, away up northward, in the direction the storm came, we hear a voice. We answer and wait. Here they come, in each other's embrace, laughing and chatting only as newly married lovers can. They were unhurt, and agreed in their story: "When the cyclone struck, the roof went, and we were drawn out at the top of the building. Away we went holding together, and on our way got in company with the wagon-body. How far we went before we struck the earth, we do not know; but it did not hurt us, though we could not stop when we came to the ground. We traveled on for awhile, sometimes up and sometimes down, until the wind got so it would let us stop; but we never saw the wagon-body any more after we came to the ground." Every house in the vicinity, seven in number, I believe, was torn to pieces; yet, strange as it may appear, not one human being, so far as I learned, received a mortal wound.

But I must tell you about my poor frightened George. I had put him in a little stable in the evening. After I found the family were safe, I thought of him; but the stable, with the bottom log, and every rail of the lot, were so clean gone that I could not mark the spot. Poor fellow! I found him next morning about two miles away, but not yet quieted in his nerves—yet as glad to see me as I was to see him. "It was a happy meeting."

ON AN INDIAN TRAIL.

From a mountain peak, toward the head waters of Denton Creek, at a distance of fifteen miles, I had an appointment. The route for twelve miles lay through the cross woods country, with no beaten track, only a pathway sufficiently distinct, when once learned, to be followed on horseback. I usually traveled this distance of mornings, early enough to meet the eleven o'clock hour. On one occasion, when I had approached to within four miles of my destination, along a glade, directly in my front, I saw a dozen or more men, armed and mounted, moving cautiously along, closely observing the ground, with occasional glances in different directions. I hastily came up to them, and found they were the citizens for whom I had an appointment at eleven o'clock. They told me they had struck the trail two or three miles back, and had been following it the way I was traveling. I saw there was no use in trying to preach that day, and therefore joined in with them, to take a lesson in an Indian hunt. In following the trail, we passed within a few hundred yards of the house in which I had an appointment for the day.

It was an easy matter to tell the tracks made by the Indians from those made by the white people, for instead of boots and shoes, they wore a heelless, round-toed moccasin. This made an impress readily recognized by all frontiersmen as an Indian sign. However, two or three in this marauding party wore shoes or boots, as was evinced by their tracks. These were regarded as white men who had banded themselves with the Indians in order that they might prey with them on the honest labors of the settlers. They adopted the Indian manners of painting and costume, except as to their feet. In the excursions of the whites against the Indians, some of this class have been killed, whence their identity became known. Against these, frontiersmen cultivated greater hatred than against the Indians themselves. It appeared strange how the Indians could slip into the country, and understand it so well, until it was found that a few white men had allied themselves with them. These could leave the country of the

Indians, put on the garb of the whites, and spend a week or two in spying out a settlement, and the range of the best herds. They could then report back, and guide the Indians in. They always came in afoot.

These moccasin people use much art to conceal their ingress. I saw myself how they would use care to evade the softer grounds; and in crossing roads they would throw down wisps of grass, a rock or chunk, and step on these, evading all possible ways of impressing the soil with their feet. But I must go on with our Indian hunt. We followed the trail until night. It was a slow business. Sometimes we would lose the trail and be detained. In all, we made eight miles that day, from the point I came up with the party. Night came on. We could do nothing more than to watch and guard, as best we could, until another day. It was a fact, the Indians were in the country. It was a night of suspense to the hardy settlers. Early the next morning, a courier from eight miles below came in hot haste, stating that there was the wildest excitement in that section; that the Indians began about two hours before day, and were collecting all the horses in the settlement. There, in an unexpected place, the Indians had inflicted their blow on the settlers, and before the sun had fairly risen, were on their way toward their haunts with about one hundred and fifty horses. They always go out in a hurry, traveling with their booty from five to eight miles an hour. Our party, on getting this news, made an effort to intercept them, but failed, by two hours. The trail they made with this vast herd was not hard to follow. I never saw men more anxious to catch villains than our party. Even I myself felt some anxiety for the prey. We pressed our horses hard in the pursuit. Quite a number of the horses, as we suppose, straggled, and there being no time to keep them in the main herd, were left. These we called "recaptured." We came on several killed, with arrows remaining in them.

But it was an unlucky day for us. By noon we had passed through the main woodland, and came to the open prairie. We could see for a long distance, but nothing of these rogues, nor of the herd they had stolen. We were probably not gaining. About two oclock, it became evident that we would have to give up the chase, for several of our party were lagging on account of their horses. A halt was made till the rear came up. A consultation was held, in which it was agreed that nothing could be effected. They returned home, and I in the direction of my next appointments. It was not a pleasant feeling to the party to go back in this plight, yet we had to make the most of it, and be content, for we had done all we could. This is just such luck as the settlers generally had with this treacherous race.

THE BROTHER WHO WAS GOING TO MAKE ME A NICE PRESENT.

For these missions there was an appropriation about half equal to a very meager support. There were a few people scattered here and there who were able to pay liberally to the support of the ministry. Some of these felt their ability, and their consciences would not let them alone when the preacher was about. They would make large promises to him once in about every six weeks. One of these, who perhaps through modesty would prefer not to have his name called here, I shall call attention to particularly, because he was not like some people I have known, but, as I think, carried out fully all his intended liberality. The young preacher always thanks God, and feels encouraged, when he meets with one of these open-hearted, good-natured, liberal men, of whom only a few are to be found in any district. But if the brethren could only realize how much good such good souls do the pastor, and especially the young preacher, their number would certainly be increased without delay.

This brother of whom I am going to tell you was very gentlemanly and kind in his house. I could not help loving him. It was early in the spring of my mission work that he told me that he liked my preaching, and that he also liked me as a man; that I was having a rough time, and doing much sacrifice in preaching the gospel to the people in those parts. He said that he thought I ought to be liberally rewarded in a temporal sense; that he felt a consciousness that I would get a rich reward for all these labors when the Master called me from labor to rest. He concluded by saying: "You may confidently expect a very handsome present from me at least." "Very well," said I, "you can do, my brother, as you find in your heart, and thank you."

Let me repeat, it makes the young preacher feel

happy, and like he is at home, to meet up with one of these full-souled, open-hearted, charitable characters, which are to be found only now and then on missions and circuits. What would become of the young preachers, if it were not for one of these? Where could they find rest? Where else could they find a model to hold up before their congregations worthy of emulation? Neither lapse of time nor change of circumstances can wash from the memory of the young preacher such a father in Israel. When I came around again, this brother reminded me of the present he was going to prepare for me. He had not forgotten it, as I feared he might. No, God bless his large soul, he was not the man that forgets when he makes promises. Ah! I could say now to my soul: "Be easy, be patient, just bide your time; give the liberal, good souls of earth their own time; that which is in a man's heart will come out, though he delays." Nor did I have to wait much longer before I realized what a big heart this brother had.

I was making my last round in that section of the work, and I concluded I would go home with my open-hearted, charitable friend; for a warm affection had sprung up between us. In bidding adieu to the people in that section of the country, I wanted to feel his hand last, from which the warm blood flowed to a warmer heart. How pleasantly our conversation flowed! But time was up with me, and I said: "My good brother, it is hard we have to break up these friendships, so far as beholding each other's faces. But I must go, and where I shall be sent only the Lord knows; but it is a blessed thought that by and by, if we are faithful, we shall obtain a rest where there are no more partings." "That is so, that is so," responded he; "and God bless you, my brother! Take this with you, and remember me. I wish I could do more for you; but this is the best I can do for you now. Times are closing down hard on me just now." "Thank you," said I, as I received the long talked of and expected present, neatly wrapped up in paper. I dropped it down in my pocket and rode away.

I had not gone far before I felt a longing desire to see the present my friend and brother had made me—his appreciation of the gospel—the value he had returned for it that year. I unrolled it carefully, and lo! there it was sure enough, sizing up with his good soul—*a plug of tobacco;* not one of your little plugs that would show up a narrow soul, but one of good size, about as big a gift as a man can get in one piece. "Ah!" thought I, "how foolish was I for once thinking this good friend and brother would forget me! Never, no." And then again, this plug of tobacco must have cost my good friend at least twenty-five cents.

I thought I would try a *cut* of it. I gave it a twist or two with my tongue, and then brought my molars down on it; but O hush! my good friend and brother was deceived. But he was not to blame. I know he, in the purity of his heart and in the goodness of his soul, did not intend to palm off on me a worthless rotten stuff with a beautiful wrapping leaf. No, the merchant deceived him, and he is the one to be blamed. Thus it is often the case in life: we mean to do good, but like my friend and brother with his tobacco-plug present, we have been imposed on ourselves. Here we hold up one man who, though disappointed by hard times, gave as much as he intended from the first. And I believe there are a few on almost every mission and circuit who emulate his example.

OUT AND IN THE COMPASS OF THE GOSPEL.

I was traveling away up toward Red River, and finding I had a little spare time, I resolved on going to a neighborhood not far off, and give them a touch of our gospel. I made inquiry, and soon found the place. Being among them, and beginning an acquaintance, I accordingly left an appointment at my next round. I came to time, and found a congregation of twenty or more people, looking just about the same as other people along on the frontier. My text that day carried me out on the love and mercy of God. I probably did not restrain myself within its legitimate scope; but having the fault, in common with many young preachers, of largely speculating, I scattered too much—shot wide of the mark, and therefore did no good. In order to show up the love and mercy of God, I gave reasons why I believed the lower animals will have a hereafter; that the love and mercy of God would induce him to provide a place for them. My soul seemed to swell with large ideas of love and mercy, and I rode out into an open sea on these tides. I did not think at the time that I was doing harm—I had no intention of it; I felt just the other way; I did not apprehend that a scowl was gathering on the brows of my audience; yet I must admit I crippled myself badly with those people that day. I knew nothing of it at the time. The family I went home with, however, I saw plainly were not pleased with the discourse. They were Baptists, and I thought ought to be pleased, for not one word had I spoken against that honorable Christian denomination; yet I had mixed the ointment with a dead fly in it; at least it appeared so to those people, and I believe to all of them without an exception. This was it: I had spoken of the probable future life of the lower orders. This was my crime, in their estimation, and I had to pay the penalty they assessed. I told this family that I was stating only what is probable, and that the thought comes up more from our rational mind and sympathies than from any direct revelation; and that many good people believe it. They insisted, however, that they did not like to be classed with the brutes that perish; and furthermore, that they did not believe that it was any part of a preacher's business in his pulpit administrations to mix up people, dogs, and cats all together; and I have thought so myself ever since; for when I had gone a long way from that place, a brother handed me a note which, when I had opened, I found to read as follows:

Dear Sir: You will please not come to our school-house to preach any more. We do not want to hear you, and we do not think our dogs and cats understand you.

This note had two signatures from that vicinity. My eyes were opened; and I thought it probably a merited rebuke. I had probably been running too fast, and resolved to check my speed. I believe I was converted; at least in the pulpit I have never since argued the immortality of the *brutes*, but have tried to keep myself within the limits of the gospel to man, which I have always found profitable and interesting to the people. I believe there is too much semi-rationalistic, speculative preaching in the world. If the merited rebuke could be given to a thousand preachers in our land who are wasting their energies on profitless views, so as to induce them to turn their shafts and spend their energies within the legitimate compass of the gospel, the progress of Christianity would be far more rapid.

The Tongue—James iii. 3–8.

On a pleasant stream on these missions lived a family who had enough of this world's goods to be happy. There was the father and mother, surrounded by several kind-hearted, bright-eyed little children who looked softly toward each other and the stranger, whoever he was, that entered. There was but one thing lacking to make this one of the happiest of families. They had enough and something to spare. The husband was intelligent; they were both Methodists; but they lacked peace at home. The husband loved the children, and I believe he loved his wife, though I could not see why, for she was one of the most caustic of women. The wife was kind enough to the children; cared diligently for the way-worn traveler, and always kept the peace when her husband was away; but from the moment he came in, there was no more peace until he left—not that he quarreled, for I never heard him speak an unkind word, or give a cross, revengeful look. I believe this wife loved her husband, notwithstanding. Her words never indicated love when he was present, yet when absent she always spoke tenderly and kindly of him. When he was away, she always appeared anxious for his return. He looked like he desired to be in, though he was mostly away, whether business called him or not. He was the worst hen-pecked man I ever saw; he was the embodiment of forbearance. He may once have tried to choke her tongue off. If he did, he lost the victory; hence he resigned himself to his fate, and resolved to endure. If we are to credit Plato, Xantippe loved Socrates; yet that old philosopher had much to endure for that love's sake.

When a man's marriage is unfortunate, I have observed that it affects him one way or another, according to his temper or inclination. Socrates looked on the subject more philosophically than most men since his day. When reproached for not driving so bad a woman from his house, I think he did not mean altogether an irony when he said he endured such a woman patiently at home so that being accustomed he would not be affected by them when abroad. But every man is not a philosopher. Some look immediately for a divorce; some go off to unknown parts; some take to intoxicants. But this man became remarkably fond of sleep. He adopted this as the happiest way of spending his time when in. It was well enough too—much better than quarreling with a wife, or of reeling under intoxicants. When he came in from the weary labors of the day, he got no words of cheer from her who had taken him "for better or for worse" in life's copartnership. He reported none of his arduous labors, none of his mishaps and trials, for he knew he would get no sympathizing, kindly spoken word to make him feel that his yoke is easy and the burden light. There met him no pleasant smile that takes away the tired man's weariness.* He fled early from the old hearth-stone to a pillow to rest his weary head. Retiring early, any one would reasonably suppose he would be an early riser; but this was not the case with this man, who chose to sleep through policy. His rising was late, extremely late for one living in the country. But by and by he is up, and quietly moves around. He loves peace, and never tells a child to wake up ma; no, he loves these moments of bliss. She was a sleeper too, especially in the morning. Why she could sleep so, and lose so much time before her husband could get out into the general business of the day, I never could tell. I know it was not her will. Probably it required all this time to recuperate her exhausted powers. But the day is not yet begun; it was never counted fairly so, until she had shaken slumber from her eyes; then one glance at her husband showed her the text of the day. I have seen many a woman, and have marked their qualities in passing along, but this one was the greatest shrew of them all. In her, on the ground that the heathen idea of metempsychosis be true, had returned the soul of Mrs. Socrates.

O the tongue, the tongue! what an unruly evil it is when unbridled! "Behold, we put bits in the horses' mouths, that they may obey us; and we turn about their whole body. Behold also the ships, which though they be so great, and are driven of fierce winds, yet are they turned about with a very small helm, whithersoever the governor listeth. Even so the tongue is a little member, and boasteth great things. Behold, how great a matter a little fire kindleth! And the tongue is a fire, a world of iniquity: so is the tongue among our members, that it defileth the whole body, and setteth on fire the course of nature; and it is set on fire of hell. For every kind of beasts, and of birds, and of serpents, and of things in the sea, is tamed, and hath been tamed of mankind: but the tongue can no man tame; it is an unruly evil, full of deadly poison."

Necessity the Mother of Invention.

The small dwellings of the missions often worked a great inconvenience. The advantages of courting especially lacked completeness. Many a young man had to postpone what he had in his heart for a more suitable occasion than was offered at the time. It seemed to me that courting under the circumstances was a very awkward business, and I wondered that so many people got married. I will now relate a case which my own eyes saw, showing how a young man was put to invention in order to get a chance to tell the idol of his heart how much he loved her. I had already observed that he was restless, and that the general conversation was not the kind he desired. I had not perceived, however, that he was so deeply absorbed in one idea. At last he had a thought; it was a bright one—a thought of policy. Said he: "Parson, can you sing?" "Not much," said I. "O I do love singing so much!" said he. "I do wish you would sing for us a little." Said I: "If you will join in and help me, I shall not object to singing myself; for I am fond of music as well as yourself, but such as I always make unassisted I have never admired." "I can't sing to do any good," said he; "however, I will help you all I can." I thought he had proposed fair enough; so I began to sing one of our songs of Zion. But look yonder! that strategic young man of the West has moved closer to his *amica deliciæ*. I sing on as though I had taken no notice of his action. Who has a heart so hard that he wouldn't give a young man a chance when in such a strait? It is but kindness and charity which should dwell in the soul, so I sung on, and they chattered on. I was not fond of the music, but I knew they were fond of the opportunity it afforded; so was I, for it looked a little funny. Young Methodist preachers are not generally so grave but that occasionally they indulge in bits of pleasant humor. I was determined the enjoyment should not all be on their side. But the song is finally finished, and with it their chattering. They glance about with rather foolish, absent looks. But this tyro of Cupid comes at me again: "Fine, fine, parson!" said he; "I do think you have such a splendid voice. Will you please sing for us again?"

Away I went again with another of our hymns, but I fear not with religious veneration. He moved his chair a little closer, and the chattering was renewed; only she talked less, half hung her head down with a semi-o'possum grin on her face. I knew she was more than half pleased; but still she fain must study a little. It is fashionable, and fashion is imperial; though no doubt her mind was made up long ago. But by and by my voice ceases to sound in music strains. "Better, better still, isn't it, Miss Mat?' said this hero at his game, and continuing, said: "I think the parson sings so well. I hope, sir, you will favor us with another song, for it is splendid." Who wouldn't sing for such a nice, appreciative young man? It would, indeed, be a hard heart that would not show charity and pulsate in sympathy. Yes, I sung for him again; but by the time I had finished, they had very much ceased to talk, and were looking with thoughtful, meditative eyes into a bright, blazing fire. The work, as I supposed, was finished. He appeared to be absent-minded; for he neither praised my last singing nor asked me to sing again. He had stormed the fort and ravished a heart under the music of the singing parson, who the old ladies said never could sing. Two faiths were plighted; two hearts were united in one; they only had to wait an opportune day to execute the nuptials. Whether ever afterward my voice was so musical to him, I know not, but rather think it was not.

I went on my way around the missions; but on my return, this young man came to me and requested that I should perform the matrimonial service. He stated that I was the choice of both, and that they had postponed wedlock, waiting for my return. When I told him I could not do it—being not yet ordained—he looked sorrowful. "But come, now," said I, "be an honest man; did you not fix up this business the day I sung for you?" "Well, parson," said he, "I reckon I shall have to confess."

A Singular Phenomenon.

I take no pleasure in carrying my narrative into the marvelous, and shall not do it any farther than the scenes and incidents of the missions will bear me out. There are now living witnesses to what I am about to relate. I give it a place in my narrative, because it is true, every word of it. It was Sunday. I had preached at eleven o'clock in Brother Jones's neighborhood, whose name I have already given such a conspicuous place. Following it up, I had a twilight appointment, for the same day, six or eight miles to the south-west. On my arrival, which was some time before night, I found a Methodist preacher, recently from Arkansas, and a Presbyterian preacher, from some miles distant, had united their efforts and were holding a protracted-meeting at the place. A brush-arbor had been built against the side of a dwelling, so that a preacher standing in the door could talk to the people in the house and under the arbor at the same time.

I told those brethren that inasmuch as I would have to be going the next day, just to go on with their meeting, conduct it to the best of their judgment, and that I would not interfere with them. But they insisted earnestly that I should fill my appointment for the evening. I felt a deep seriousness and a strong desire to do good, for these brethren had already, through grace, worked up a deep seriousness among the people. Our lights were but dimly burning, yet it was a beautiful starlight night. I preached with unusual liberty, as much as I had ever experienced, or more perhaps. The congregation appeared attentive and solemn. All of a sudden, and most unexpectedly, there shone a soft light. It came with a sudden flash and then gradually died away. I suppose from first to last it occupied four or five seconds. Every face of the audience instantly became distinctly visible, as if lit up with phosphorescent rays. Many of the people sprung to their feet, and there was a general staring gaze and cry of wonder from the people all around, both in the house and under the arbor. It affected both saint and sinner. The occasion was one of awful solemnity. As it went off, the congregation appeared to be bathed in tears, and overcome almost to helplessness. I felt much overawed and overcome myself at the strange sight. I called for penitents. They came, and bowed where they were. It was the only occasion I ever saw in which everybody wanted religion, and was publicly striving for it. For awhile there was no singing, no exhorting, no leading any way in regular order. But by and by the spell on the people began to break and the people to govern themselves, but still with deep solemnity.

Now, I have simply given the facts appertaining to this strange phenomenon. I have only a few times mentioned it to any one, because of the existing incredulity the world has for such things. I once since saw a sight which I think furnishes a key that unlocks the mystery. It was also on a beautiful starlight night. A light shone suddenly all about me, and the whole section of the country appeared to be lit up by it. It gradually, and not suddenly, died away. When it first flashed on my vision, I threw my eyes toward the sky, and there directly in front of me, at an angle of about fifty degrees, was the plainly visible track of a blazing meteor, which had not yet finished its course. It burned with less and less brilliancy until it ceased to blaze altogether, and then the long glowing line it left gradually died away. It was a good reminder of the phenomenon that appeared on the night of the meeting referred to. I am inclined to think this was the way of it; and thus it may be accounted for on natural principles.

Granting this view of the subject to be true, that meteor would no doubt have fallen that night at the same time and place, and marked the same line in its passage, had there been no meeting appointed. The people might have all been in their beds, and the phenomenon passed unobserved; or some lone traveler might have been the only witness, and could tell the people the strange sight he saw. But however it may be, one thing I do earnestly believe, and that is that God often turns the happenings of nature to good account. A little superstition is sometimes favorable to godliness, and I shall not be surprised if in eternity the fact is revealed that some souls were saved through the phenomenon of that night.

Mischievous Turn to Call the People Out.

I am no strategist, yet I know many of other denominations and some of our own who are. They study well the policy of calling the people out to their meetings. They make many strategic movements. They are best known as sensationalists. The preacher who gets the most people to hear him does not always do the most good. He may have the power of awakening the curiosity and novelty of the people, by announcing his subjects beforehand, and yet the whole of the proceedings may not be accompanied with the solemnity and reverence due the worship of Almighty God. Whether it be proper or not to announce subjects generally beforehand, is an open question. One thing we do know—it was not the apostolic manner, nor did Christ command it. However, in my young ministerial days, while out on the missions, I tried it once, and only once. I believe I had occasion which required it.

At one of my appointments, rather a dense settlement, and quite in from the border, the people would not come out to meeting—only a few, very few. This was harassing to the young preacher, of course, who always thinks he has something to say that everybody ought to hear. This notion I had not yet outlived, and therefore I began to cast about how I should manage to get the people out to hear me. Finally, I resolved on announcing a strange subject, and give them a touch of sensationalism. Accordingly, I announced to them that "at my next regular round a stranger to many of them would preach on the subject of the first murderer." The few that were there looked at each other and whispered a little, on the mere announcement. I only added: "Important subject. Please make it known in the neighborhood." To all their inquiries about "who is he going to preach on that subject, and who was the first murderer," I only answered, "Just be patient, wait and see."

An old lady remarked, rather knowingly, that she knew who was the first murderer. "Why, he was Cain; for he killed his brother; and they belonged to the first family." Being afraid this view of the old lady might lull them into quiet on the subject, I remarked that "the man who would preach at my next round denied that." "Well," said she, "I do not know who on earth it can be, if it was n't Cain, for I never heard of Adam killing anybody; but I 'll hear him anyhow when he comes, and if I ain't right, then I 'll know."

I saw it was a "hit." I left them, and was so occupied that I thought little more of it until I had come around again to within a few days of the place. I then reviewed my subject, which I had been at some pains to prepare for the occasion. I intended to do my best, and build up, if possible, a good congregation; for there had in those days crept into me that which slyly creeps into most young preachers during their first years—a large idea of personal ability and merit; and if the people would only come out, see it, and be convinced, there would never be vacant seats when they preached.

At last the day came, the hour; and as I came in sight I saw what I had never seen before at that place—horses hitched all about; more horses and more people than I thought were in that country. Said a brother to me, as I stepped to the door of the little log school-house: "I thought a man was going to preach here to-day on the subject of the first murderer." I responded: "I think he will; hasn't he come?" And as I passed on, I heard him say, "Not as I have seen." I lost no time; I knew it wouldn't do. I went down into my "treasury department," and was at it before the people could think.

My text was John viii. 44: *"He was a murderer from the beginning."* When I read the text, there was a general look that told plainly they were sold. No people can bear a good joke or keep their equipoise better, under such circumstances, than the people in the West. If any one had got mad, I would have had no fighting to do; for many would have taken my part. It is far the best always to take a joke in good humor. Of course I said nothing of the context which might perhaps apply to them. The "ye" I left out entirely, and confined myself strictly to the person contained in the text—"the first murderer," the devil. After descanting on his fighting Michael, and other probable evil deeds he had wrought in the moral universe, I took rather a Miltonic view of his entry into our world, and how on account of his agency sin has corrupted every heart. In conclusion, I exhorted them to make a good warfare against the evil machinations of this first and greatest murderer in the universe; to obey the injunction of the apostle, and not "forsake the assembling of themselves together, as the manner of some is;" that in this course there is safety.

As I passed out, a good-natured elderly gentleman took me by the hand and said: "Well, my friend, ain't you going to announce for us again." "Not this time," said I, and went on. But may be you want to know if my congregation kept up at that place. I answer it did; at least for one more appointment, for it was never my good luck to meet with those people but once more, which was at my next regular round. I was greeted with a large congregation and treated with most courtly manners. The year was drawing to a close. This was my first effort at sensationalism. Though it resulted well, yet I must say I am not fond of such experiments.

The Strait of the Young Preacher in Administering a Reproof.

This is one of the hardest duties the preacher is ever called on to perform. He should bear patiently and much before he attempts it. Yet it sometimes becomes necessary. When this is the case, it should be done tenderly, in love, and in such a Christian spirit as to make the guilty party heartily ashamed of himself, and not hate the preacher. I have known most uncharitable rebukes to fall from the lips of those whom I regarded as good men. The fruit that followed was the extremest hate.

In the West, my patience was never much taxed on this score. The people there generally behave well when at a religious meeting. They are every whit as orderly as in the older States. If I wanted to find order in religious assemblies, veneration for the service, and respect for God, I would never leave the trans-Mississippi department of the United States to find it. Yet cases do sometimes occur, and should be reproved. When they are a necessity, the preacher should have courage to exercise his prerogative under the law and his duty in the proper spirit. But the trouble with me in those days, as I suppose, was the same as that with most young preachers. It breaks the line of thought, and therefore tends to disaster. Indeed, in those days, I had no time for it, and dreaded the rising occasion.

The subject to whom I shall call your attention was a little girl who thought she was grown, and frisked about on her seat and talked at a wonderful rate. She was the veriest imp of a disturber I have ever met. May be she was grown; at least she thought she was. But she was small, very small for a grown lady. The subject of my discourse was an important one; at least I thought it was more than ordinarily so. It was on this account that I was as anxious for the people to hear as this little disturber was to frisk about on her seat and talk. Her maneuvering, however, divided the attention of the people. I wanted to shut her mouth and keep her quiet on her seat, but I was so poised on my subject that I had no time to administer a reproof in words. It just seemed to me that I could not stop without suffering a disaster. But still that little mouth had to stop, and that frisking motion must become quiet. While profoundly absorbed in the thought and labor of my sermon, I began slowly and unconsciously to move out in my congregation, until I found myself directly in front of this troublesome little girl. I was still poised on my subject, though full twelve feet from my proper place, throwing the gospel directly into her face with all the vehemence of my soul, as though this was the fort Satan had erected, and that should be stormed—this his stronghold to be pulled down. The reproof was successful. The stream of her words ceased, and she sat like a statue. I gradually worked myself back to my proper place, so that by the time the discourse was finished, the minds of the hearers were distracted from both the young lady and my own manner of administering a reproof.

It all presents to my mind now a touch of the novel. It is by no means a manner I have kept up. I would not recommend it. It sprung as a spontaneity out of the straitened mental state of the young preacher. It was not in this instance without its proper good fruit. It made a well-behaved young lady out of that rude girl. It did more for her than all the dancing-schools in the land—more than all the semi-barbarous notions of etiquette that have been introduced into civilization. Before I left the missions, she became a member of the Church, along with her parents.

The Stiff Preacher.

The people in the West, and especially on these missions, were remarkable for their plainness of speech as well as of dress. They kept themselves decent enough, but were altogether careless about fashion. They detested nothing more than a stiff manner, puffed-up look, or self-arrogance. They liked pliability in a man—one who could adapt himself without trouble or apparent restraint to existing circumstances. The business of the preacher, as they regarded it, was to convert them from their vices to Christ. This they liked in him. But to reproach them for their manners was like invading with an evil eye their most sacred precincts. It built a wall of partition between him and them, and of course put an end to his usefulness among them. A preacher laboring among such people must of necessity study adaptability. Should he go with the faint semblance of imperialism, he will find himself soon ousted. He need not sacrifice proper etiquette and become rude. No; he may labor with them for a year, and, if any thing, come out improved in manners, for he is sure to be improved in understanding. He may often find a warm heart bound round with a buckskin coat, or a broad brain covered with a wolf-skin cap. They only want a man to lay aside the unnecessary and troublesome etiquette of the age, along with its false ideas. They love true politeness, the conventionalities built on a broad common sense, but detest nothing more than false appearances. The influence of some preachers in the

West has been destroyed because they were artless in adaptation.

I will illustrate this case now in hand by an anecdote. A preacher whom I knew, and who had traveled a portion of the work before I had, made his mark with some of the people, and especially with an old-like lady. Alluding to his predecessor, said she, "Do you know preacher B——?" "Yes," said I, "he and I are well acquainted." "Where does he live?" said she. I answered, designating the place. Said she, "Where was he raised?" I gave the place. "Isn't he rich?" said she. I answered, "No, but he has a competency." "Is there any thing the matter with his back?" said she very inquiringly, as though I could give the required information by my intimate acquaintance with him. I answered: "No; I have never heard there was any thing the matter with his back. But why do you ask me all these questions of Brother B——?" "Because," said she, "he is the stiffest man that ever visited these parts."

How the Young Preacher Got Cheated Out of a Sermon.

A young preacher has sometimes to pay for his carelessness, and profit by the lesson. I remember once being in very ill luck and cleverly cut out of a sermon on this account: I had got in on Saturday evening where I was to preach on Sunday. The morning in the early part of the day proved to be rather rainy—just such as in the West would entice one to put on some of his worst clothes. On account of the rain and a little exposure in it, I had put on an alpaca so worn and abused by age that the wonder with me now is why I had it along at all; but I had it somehow stowed away in my "treasury department," and had that morning pulled it out from its "lurking-place." I became meditative, and thought no more of it.

At last the hour came for preaching, and I arose in the dwelling where I staid all night, and was before my audience, feeling impressed with the importance of my subject and its great worth to human souls. Slowly, solemnly, and with measured emphasis, I announced my text: "Now abideth faith, hope, charity; these three; but the greatest of these is charity." Just at the close of this announcement, I happened to look down, and saw my seedy old alpaca. Then began the struggle as to whether I would preach or not. In very small things are sometimes involved great issues and mighty struggles. The movements of an insect nerved again the heart of one of Scotland's chiefs, and led the way to glorious triumph; but this was leading to inevitable and inglorious failure; and yet the gospel is just as important as Scotch liberty. I thought, "Surely my congregation will think I am begging," for the old alpaca was openly before their eyes as an index-finger, with its brown age, rents and shreds, pointing to the thoughts in my mind. Well, for once I felt that I either had the wrong text or else the wrong coat; but how to make a change I could not tell. I was not of the Hard-shell persuasion, or else I might have pulled off the old thing and have laid it on the back of a chair, as when a boy I used to see the Baptists in Kentucky pull off their heavy mixed jean coats, when preaching on a hot summer day.

O the young preacher has so many trials and vexations! He is able to bear them and endure simply because he is young and ambitious. I thought, as I began, my congregation were indulging in a smile—not at my mental state, but at the idea of preaching charity by costume. I went on somehow or other, in a crippled way, and filled in a full half hour. I have no doubt but that day I largely emulated the example of some preachers I have seen, who neither filled in the stops with solemn stillness nor "Selah," but with clearing their throats. All my efforts to bring out the idea of love as contained in the text seemed to me fruitless, since my congregation could plainly see that it was only digging about the base on which that idea of charity in their minds stood, and out of which it grew. It made no difference in what phase I presented the text, the old alpaca stood most prominently before my eyes, and as I thought before the eyes of my congregation. When I was done, I did not know what I had said. I knew I did not say what I intended before I began.

At last I quit, feeling more as I did when I preached that remarkable sermon from the first Psalm, in the section of country where my friend "Jesse" lived, than ever at any other time. But at this place I had no friend "Jesse" to help me out by singing. There was an old lady in the congregation at this place who generally helped me to sing. If ever I needed her help, it was at this time; but she would not help me. When I dismissed the congregation, I reproached her for not helping me to sing. She added, "I do always help you when you have the tune." Although I knew I could not sing well, and was conscious that I did sometimes leave the proper tune for one of my own—always by accident, however, and not from choice—yet this remark of the old lady put the whole machinery of my being in bad working order for the remainder of the day. Her sentiment was neither romance nor poetry; yet to be so mercilessly pounded, when already murdered and dead, reminded me of the savageness of Indian rule.

But I had already learned to endure, and a little of the art of being alive when I was dead. Neither the pounding the old lady gave me nor the promise of a new coat one brother made me was sufficient to kill me entirely. A young preacher, you see, can endure a great deal after he has had time for a little training. In the revolution of my thoughts, I was satisfied that I would recover from the shock, and live to see a better day. The lesson of that day was as valuable to me as the lessons in Clark's Manual, which was in my year's course of study. It caused me to watch myself more vigilantly, not only in my dress, but also in my general deportment. I determined to look more thoroughly into the principles of music, and labor harder than ever before to improve my voice, so as to make endurable melody when singing. Some of those things which happened to me were not pleasant at the time, yet I am now glad that they came up in my history, for they were profitable lessons. We sometimes drink a bitter cup, but it cures disease.

But I cannot leave this subject without a word of adieu to the old alpaca. It is properly due to it, since it is the last one I ever wore. Our likes and dislikes of things come often from our experiences. You know the bees stung me badly once, when I was a little boy playing in the yard. On this account I could not endure their honey for many years. I never liked the spots where I had sad experiences, when a boy. I do not like alpaca coats—never wear them. Now, since I have left them off, I remember they were always too hot in summer and too cold in winter. If any young preacher wants the heat to break out on him, just let him try one a little exposed to the sun on a hot summer day. The remains of the old alpaca lie near about the spot where I failed in my sermon on charity. I never allowed it to go with me any farther on the mission work, and creep out and do mischief on rainy days.

Some Disadvantages.

Many of the people on the missions lived in small houses—very small, often but one room. I often thought they ought to do better. They, many of them at least, could have done much better than they did. A single room for cooking, eating, warming, and sleeping, with a rather numerous household, was certainly not pleasant to the family, if at all cultivated, and far less so to the stranger who was compelled to seek shelter for the night; yet sometimes even the stranger and weary traveler thanked God for the comforts such a place afforded. In the West, of course the young preacher always did the best he could for himself; yet, notwithstanding his best efforts to find accommodation, he was bound to deem himself unfortunate.

I will give but a single view of the disadvantages among many on these missions; and from this index inference may be drawn of the strait into which many poor but decent people were sometimes forced, and the consequent punishment they endured. They visited the same as the people in the older settlements. Many of them washed themselves, put on clean clothes, and looked decent on Sunday. Just think of Sunday morning coming, and the young men wanting to appear clean and in their best suits before their "sweethearts!" Now, watch them prepare, will you? Perhaps a Texas blue Norther is blowing. Such a thing is neither uncommon nor unlikely. They stand prominently among the many happenings of the West. These young men, called "boys," may wash, and even have warm water, at the door of the little cabin home; but see them now again going off, each with a white shirt and his Sunday suit on his arm. Where are they going? Either to a place under the hill or, which is more likely, to the shedded rail-pen—there, when the thermometer is half way to zero, to strip and shiver until the untidy garb of a week's wear can be exchanged for a brighter suit, one that will be very pleasing to those whom their hearts delight to see. This is no fancy sketch, nor is the picture overdrawn. Now, this way of doing seems to be a necessity with some, yet only a few in comparison with the number who indulge in it. As I have remarked, most of them could do much better. How so many could live years and years this way, without mending or trying to mend their ways, was always a wonder to me. I do not indorse the old adage that "it takes all kinds of people to make the world," but I believe about all kinds are in it; but some of the kinds not of necessity.

The Ungoverned Family.

To have to live on a puncheon floor will remind the old people of this day of the stories their fathers told them of pioneer days in some of the older States. Under such disadvantages the people could not be as comfortable, nor as easily train their children to good manners, as when circumstances are more favorable; yet many could have done much better than they did, notwithstanding all the disadvantages of frontier life. I remember spending a night once with a family which lived eastward of the missions, the father of which was a man of some pretensions, and for many years had been a licensed preacher, but had never graduated to orders. He had a remarkable library for a man of his class, though he never read it—thinking to have knowledge in his house was sufficient, without the trouble of getting it into his brain. He was often guilty of a half-spitting, silly laugh through his teeth, which when once seen by sensible people always marked him as a man whose inherent possibilities would never raise him above the plane of a very common man. Yet he was honest and compromising to a fault; a blacksmith by trade, as well as a preacher;

allowing his customers to say how much they should pay him for the work he did for them, which in many cases was a very meager sum—not enough to raise him off the inimitable rickety puncheon floor on which he was raising his rather numerous family. His preaching of course was not wise, yet a few people, silly like himself, bragged on him; which, however, never reached his own ears without inducing the silly laugh, that all decent people like to avoid.

This man's compromising spirit entered largely into his own household arrangements; for the man who had not the courage to assess his customers and vindicate the claims of his muscle would naturally lack the courage to correct his own children. Though they had a father, yet they had to be reared without one; for to the eye of the visitor or stranger, they, the father and the children, all appeared to be boys together, enjoying equal rights and privileges; the only discoverable difference was one was bearded and showed more the marks of age. Yet this man, true to the custom of a preacher, held his family prayers; for he had a heart, though not a way, to be obedient in the Church, and to rear his "children in the nurture and admonition of the Lord." No doubt many funny and some sad and lamentable things happened, and as quickly were forgotten, in his family worship, and other attempts at family government, as is illustrated in the following account.

As I said, I was with this family once for a night. I felt pained in my heart when I saw the mixed way in which parents and children got along. I thought he needed the severest rebuke, and that power to govern should be driven into him some way, even though it might appear after a sledge-hammer fashion, like an Irishman driving spikes into railroad ties; but being young myself, I did not deem it proper to appear in the office of such an administrator. But the hour arrived for prayers, and of course I had to lead. Things went on well enough until we bent our knees in worship, for I, being a stranger, was a sort of novelty to the family of children, who on this account took up more time in gazing, and therefore put in less with their capers. But early in our prayer a rat had found its way up through the puncheon floor into the room where we were all on our knees, and found it very difficult to get back again. The boys were always ready, and never lost an opportunity when there was a chance for amusement or fun. They had sufficient training not to forget they were at prayers, and no one presumed to get off his knees. The rat in the room was intensely exciting to the boys. They took all liberty in the chase except to get off their knees. The first large whisper I heard was, "Dick, did you stop the hole?" Then commenced the sport with the boys in earnest. Hear them: "There he comes, Joe; catch him!" "Look out, Ben; I seen him there by you!" "Run him this way, Dick; I'll fix him!" These and such like loud whispers go round and round. At the same time they pushed their chairs and ran on their knees. Nor did it cease until about the time the "amen" was pronounced, at which time the rat had found his way out again. I did expect for once that this father would give those, as I regarded, not rude but neglected boys a solemn lecture; but not a word fell from his lips to them. He looked toward me, and with his silly laugh through his teeth, remarked: "Did n't the boys get into a tantrum?" Whether this brother was right or not in his use of the word *tantrum*, I did not stop to discuss. It was not now a question over a word, but of principle. There was a spirit of manhood in me, and it was rising to meet this emergency. Though no general sermon-reader, yet I remembered that Wesley had a sermon on family government. I knew he had Wesley's sermons in his library. Said I: "My brother, will you have patience to hear me read a sermon?" He said he would. I then drew down from the shelf the book, and read to him Wesley's sermon on training children. When I finished it, I simply added: "My brother, you are neglecting your children, and they may come to ruin." The wife of this man had been patient through all the proceedings until now. I saw she was anxious and determined to say something, and I was in dread lest she might turn her tongue on me for the liberty I used toward her husband, and that I would have to look like a galley-slave. But no; in this I was disappointed most agreeably. Said she, turning her eyes on her husband: "Wesley is right, and you are wrong. I have told you for a long time these boys would be hanged some day; and that will be a sad time to you, when you know that you will be the cause of it. I have tried and tried to govern them, but I cannot govern them by myself, and there is just no use in trying any longer. You have just got to govern, or else you will find trouble ahead." Here the good wife broke down with her closing remarks, as women sometimes do. She was evidently fretted, and saw full well the folly and danger of neglect in family government. The husband held his head-down like a repenting sinner. Even the children for once looked solemn. I verily believe if a rat had obtruded on the puncheon floor it would not have broken the stillness.

It was an occasion, such as one might desire, to sow good seed. The ground was well prepared. I tried to make the time profitable, and as well as I remember said: "My dear brother and sister, it is not too late. Only be mutual helps to each other. Spend a few minutes each day in friendly, private talk about your children and how they should be trained. Remember the claims Heaven has on you, and how you will have to give an account for your folly and neglect. Be strict, not severe. Be parents; not like a master and mistress, domineering over your children as though they were slaves. Study well the future interest of your children, and God will bless you and help you bring them up in his nurture and admonition." These remarks closed the evening. I believe they did good. I trust with better hearts we all retired to rest. O what a power there is in words! What a stream of good or evil flows from them! Anacharsis, the Scythian, said: "Words are more vivifying than the showers of spring, and sharper than the sword of destruction." Solomon says: "A word fitly spoken is like apples of gold in pictures of silver."

Dismissing the Missions, etc.

But I at last began to close up my work on the missions, and to make preparation for the ensuing Conference. In reference to the preceding sketches and anecdotes, I must say they are as true as I have language to narrate them. My object has not been to give them a burnished or gilded appearance, but to stick closely to the facts in the case of each one, using language only clever enough not to make you weary in hearing them. Now, while such things might be continued to farther length, I propose to break the monotony, and proceed with the closing up of the mission work. I left the work organized with twenty-five appointments. A few of those taken in at first were dropped off on account of good reasons, and others were added, so that the above-named number stood at the close of the year. I had preached a little more than one hundred times after the order of my ability, and had traveled on the work, according to my best count, upward of three thousand miles. I found many warm-hearted people, and made many friends. Toward the last I felt remarkably contented with myself. I had made it a point to lose no appointment—to do the work of a preacher as best I could. In order to this, I put aside personal convenience and inclination, and went through heat and cold, well fed or hungry, housed at night in the little cabin of the frontiersman or canopied by the tent of the immigrant, preaching, traveling, visiting, talking to the children—which was always an easy and pleasant task with me; sometimes wearied, but never out of humor; sometimes wet, but always got dry again; sometimes in tears, but they always ceased to flow. Thank God for tears! a hundred times they carried me out of the darkness of night into the beautiful day-dawn.

Leaving the missions was like leaving friends again at home. I was greatly afraid I would not be sent back; yet I know not why. There was no good accommodation—not a house on the entire work built exclusively for preaching. I had not seen any thing called a pulpit since I had been out. It was, I suppose, a hard work, though I did not know it at the time. It was a place to be exposed, to sacrifice, and to suffer. Your preacher-boy was only passing through what many others were bearing at the same time. Here I learned to endure, for I had a nature that would not revolt. I became a minister of the gospel honestly, and, as I understand, in obedience to God's will. He planted me there, and only once was I tempted to desert the cause. But *he* provided for me even then. I had learned to preach after my own style now without much trouble. I had received twenty dollars solid gold missionary money. I had received along-side of this from the people—in the way of boots, hats, tobacco, and other things, with a few dollars mixed along—thirty-nine dollars and twenty-five cents. My wages received aggregated fifty-nine dollars and twenty-five cents; yet I was not discouraged, but was ready to go to Conference. I went as well clad as the average preacher, for I had plenty notwithstanding—a pleasant ranch with some increasing and growing stock, on which I could draw any day. I was prosperous, notwithstanding all my reverses.

But I will not dismiss the missions until I refer to a little circumstance by which I became convinced that I had made improvement. I had not been out on the missions long before I conceived the idea of writing a few sermons, to be used on extra occasions. Before the year closed, I had a little manuscript volume of twelve sermons. I felt very proud of these. Several of them I thought sufficiently worthy to be preached anywhere and in any place. I had drawn on that manuscript volume several times, as the year was going out. One leisure day, toward the last of the work, I thought I would do as I suppose young preachers have often done—select and prepare one of my best sermons, and hold it in readiness, laid aside; for may be I might be called on to preach at Conference. So I concluded to spend that day among the thoughts contained in my manuscript volume. I soon had it out from among the other things I had stowed away in my "treasury department," was glad of the opportunity, and opened it for a real treat. I began to read and look at the divisions I had made. I was not well pleased. I tried to reconcile my thoughts with the *status* of the manuscript, but my thoughts would be revolutionary—my mind would not endure it. I tried one sermon after another, all with the same dislike. The very things I once appreciated in them most I now thought most trifling. The sentiments I once thought necessary to give a sermon completeness, and set it off with fine, finished touches, appeared now most unworthy. I looked on, and found I was more rhetorical than profound; that I had imbibed a style too bombastic. I became thoroughly disgusted with my manuscript sermons, and my preaching generally, and longed for another round on the missions, to show the people a different and, as I thought, a better style of preaching. I felt like I wanted to correct some things, at least.

I committed that manuscript volume to the flames before the going down of the sun—was glad that it was the only copy in existence. I was now completely revolutionized in my thoughts, and I resolved to be more profound, but not less rhetorical. I think it all evinced that I had made progress in my understanding.

As is common with many young preachers, I had become a little vainglorious—thought more highly of myself than I ought; had been drinking all the sentiments of praise I could get and longing for more, not knowing that those had a tendency more to make a fool of a man than to do him good. Because some young lawyer said I could beat the presiding elder preaching, I thought surely if I had not already made my mark that I would at least be a wonderful man some day. I never failed to drink in all the words of flattery I could catch. If any one said I was a good preacher, it only confirmed the private opinion already existing in my mind. Now as I retrospect the past, it all looks like a great weakness in me. I found out years afterward that the presiding elder could beat me preaching badly; that poor judges, even though they be lawyers, and weak-minded people, praise the young preacher. I did not remember in after-years that the sensible and the wise had ever spoken words that tended to excite my vanity—only those who do not know what good preaching is, who take vehemence for doctrine, and sound for sense.

But somehow I weathered through this crisis of the young preacher, and when among my seniors I behaved as decorously as I knew how, whatever the inward consciousness I had of myself. I sometimes wondered why they did not put me up on the great occasions, and let all the people get their eyes open like a certain young lawyer, and see that I could indeed beat the presiding elder preaching. Now, my dear mother, I know you want the true history of your preacher-boy, yet some of it, you see, is not praiseworthy of him. Yet I know you have the wisdom to know the things that try the young preacher, and how narrowly he escapes many evils, and that the one who graduates to deliberate manhood and sobriety unscathed would be a marvel on the pages of history. Your preacher-boy only passed through the stages in the ministry that every mother's son in the ministry has tried. Many a young preacher, I imagine, has traveled along these paths, and has been affected by them. Many more yet unborn in the ministry will never see our foot-prints, and therefore, not knowing a way of escape, will be similarly impressed. It is well enough even for a young preacher to think well of himself, but by all means never be vainglorious and puffed up; for there is more hope for a fool than for a man who is wise in his own conceit.

ADVICE OF AN OLD PREACHER—GOING TO CONFERENCE AGAIN.

On my way to Conference, I fell in company with an old preacher, a man whom I had known from boyhood, who had found his way to Texas, and who knew something of the hardships and trials of the frontier as well as myself. He was an itinerant of experience, and therefore knew much more of Conference business and Conference appointments than I did. I had my "treasury department" with me, but felt it a little burdensome. It is true, as already observed, I had made it lighter by burning up that *weighty* volume, my manuscript sermons; yet it seemed heavy—too heavy, I thought, to be carried two hundred and fifty miles on horseback. I sympathized also with my faithful George, who had already one hundred and eighty pounds of mortality to bear, and who, notwithstanding, had never once treated me unkindly, but who, on the contrary, had been with me in perils of the Indians and in perils of the cyclone. In view of the distance, and how reasonable I thought it was to be sent back to some mission or circuit not remote from where I had been, I said to my fellow-traveler: "My brother, I believe I will lighten my *treasury;* for I think if I am not sent back to the missions I will certainly be sent back to some place in this section not very remote." This good brother, with the true foresight of a regular itinerant, in a fatherly and rather solemn manner said: "My young brother, let me give you a little advice. You are inexperienced, and do not understand Methodist economy yet. You do not know what is to become of you. It is all uncertain. You may be sent hundreds of miles the other way. Remember this is a large Conference in its territory —nearly twice as large as the State you came from. The young unmarried preacher lives on horseback more than any other. He never needs a wagon. His treasury department, as you denominate the historic saddle-bags, carries his estate of clothing and books. Carry it all along, and be ready. You will have no time to come back two hundred and fifty miles for things that are left."

I took this advice with a willing mind. I left nothing behind—was determined to go, it made no difference where; but still I thought, Surely I will be sent back somewhere not far off from where I had been traveling. I was acclimated in that part of the great Empire State. I understood the people in that section, and regarded myself adapted to them. It might impair my health to be sent into pine woodland districts, or into the southern malarial portions. These things, I thought, would be seen and looked after by the appointing authority. But when I consented to take every thing with me, I thought but little more of it.

In going to Conference this time, I felt none of the burden bearing on me and pressing me down that

I felt one year before. I had been tried, and I was fully established in the ministry. I loved it above all things. It was my meat and drink now to preach. Though I did not do it well, yet I thought I did; and in this was my enjoyment. I know I always did my best. I was greatly improved—never had learned as much in one year in all my life. It appeared like a poor chance to improve, but the work of the missions kept me fully awake. This is the proper condition of mind in which to learn. Full employment is necessary to development. My knowledge came in from all sources. I learned from observation, from conversation, through prayer, through preaching, by studying, and patient endurance. I felt quite an easy conscience, and therefore went in peace.

At Conference Again.

Meeting at Conference was a renewal of old friendships. Thank God for such reunions! How pleasant it is to see brethren dwell together in unity! How joyous the occasion when brethren meet who have not seen each other's faces for a year! How pleasant to narrate the incidents, and give sketches from life portraiture over a district of country four hundred miles across! But how exceedingly lovely to tell how through Christ we had assembled again in triumph! How rich the pleasure when no one has degraded his ministerial character—when no one has trailed Immanuel's banner!

But here is a meeting in which men are tried. Joints that are made of clay are sure to fall to pieces.

Only true metal will stand the fiery trials through which these servants of God are called to pass, and on which they are now beginning to enter. The whole public heart at this time was getting into the throes of the war between the States. It was *war, war*, and of course the Church would suffer. It was very evident that the minister had a great charitable work to do. He had to preserve the Church on poor pay. How appropriate the lesson from the presiding officer! "We are troubled on every side, yet not distressed; we are perplexed, but not in despair; persecuted, but not forsaken; cast down, but not destroyed." It was read deliberately and in solemn tone. Then the hymn—

>And are we yet alive,
>And see each other's face?—

gave unction to the occasion. Yes, we were alive who were there, but some had passed over to their rich inheritance. Others there were who would never meet on another such occasion. It all looked solemn. I felt solemn. Many an eye dropped a tear. Thank God for tears! When the body of man is dry and scorched with fever, what a relief comes when the pores of the skin are opened and nature begins again her regular work! When the soul of man is all broken and bruised, if God will only open the lachrymal canals, that it may give forth its acknowledgments through tears to him and to the world, a great relief is found. God has provided a way for the soul to sweat off its trouble—"Jesus wept." Tears came through the body, but they came from the fountain of the soul. O how I like a healthy lachrymal canal and the big sensible tear that on proper occasions comes dropping, dropping down—pouring out the state of the soul! It always makes a man feel better. But ah! a fevered body that cannot sweat, and a bowed, sorrowing spirit that cannot weep! Here is pain, here is trouble without relief. They are both subjects alike of pity.

Yet I believe the lachrymal canal may be unhealthy. Chronic tears are as bad as not to weep at all, or even worse. There are a few preachers who cannot preach for crying; some who hoist their flood-gates even when there is no pathos in their periods and little reason in their words. It is disgusting when the narrator of anecdotes does all the laughing. It is alike unpleasant when the preacher does all the weeping. That preacher does well when he can open the lachrymals of his congregation first. Then it is always legitimate for him to weep along with them, if he so desires.

Reading the Appointments.

At last the Conference came to a close. The finishing stroke always is reading the appointments. This exercise never fails to awaken deep interest. A district was called, but not the one I was from—my name is not mentioned in manning that. Just as I expected, they were saving me for the same old district. Another district is called, but my name had no connection with it. Finally the district I was from was called. Now I listened. They will put me on that somewhere, surely; but somehow they missed my name. Finally they came to next to the last district. Every place is named and filled. Still my name is left out. "What does it all mean?" thought I. "They have called all the country I ever heard of, and more too, and yet they have neither called my name nor given me a place. Have they dropped my name from the roll? Why, surely they have. I wonder if in this business they ever overlook a fellow entirely. Accidents do happen sometimes. Surely there is a big mistake somewhere." But by and by I stopped these surmisings, and waited to hear it all through—remembering a good brother as I came down, advising me to take every necessary thing with me, said, "You don't know what is to become of you." Well, I didn't. But hear. They are on the last district. Name after name is called, and a preacher is placed. Finally they are all called but one. At last the president, in a clear, sonorous voice, cries out, "Blank Station!" Another pause, as if looking to find the man, and then in a voice equally clear rang out the name of your preacher-boy; and this closed the drama of the call.

I had been in Texas for some time, but had never heard of that place. I did not know whether it was in Texas or not, but supposed it was. I said meekly to a brother sitting by me, "Do you know where that station is?" "No," said he, "I never hard of it before." I moved among the brethren making inquiries, for I did not know to which cardinal-point it lay. Finally one brother spoke up and said, "Yes, I know where it is." "Where?" said I with anxious inquiry. Said he: "Your station is away down yonder so far in Texas that if you make a step south you will drown in the Gulf of Mexico, and if you step east you leave the State entirely. It is a monstrous fishy place." I asked him if he had ever been there. He said, "No, nor do I care to." Another preacher, who I did not know was taking interest in our conversation, said: "Have courage, my young brother; you will see many novel things down there. Ships in abundance, and people from everywhere. You will get to 'see old ocean, and hear it roar.' You can spend a leisure hour now and then shooting alligators and catching fish." "Thank you, my good brother," said I; "this is comforting. I think I shall like the place. I have always had a desire to see 'old ocean.'" Another preacher, as I supposed to try me, said, "Are you going there?" I looked up at him. His lip curled a little humorously. I made him no reply, for I was not ready for such thrusts. I could not help feeling a little serious. I now fully realized the truth of the good brother's instruction: "Take all your things with you, for you do not know what is to become of you."

Thoughts—Rest—Start for the Station.

My promotion to a station reminded me very much of a remark of one of Cæsar's soldiers. When this soldier, a member of the historic Tenth Legion, was temporarily promoted to be a cavalryman for Cæsar's personal safety during the colloquy he had with Ariovistus, he humorously said: "*Plus quam pollicitus esset Cæsarem facere; pollicitum se in cohortis prætoriæ loco decimam legionem habiturum; ad equum rescribere.*" Now, I was evidently promoted, but neither as a body-guard nor cavalryman for *Cæsar*. While on the missions, I belonged to the cavalry arm of the ministry; but in the station, I supposed I would not have much use for a horse. But let us look at the character of the promotion. It was from missions to a station, from a saddle to a footman, from dry lands to much water, from the Western wilds four hundred miles south-east to city life, from all acquaintanceship to a place among strangers, from the back of a chair to a pulpit, from the cabins of the frontiersmen to comfortable dwellings, from ox-teams to steam-ships, from the time kept by a watch to the sound of a church-bell.

I slept soundly through the night, and awoke next morning much refreshed. I felt exceedingly anxious to see how things appeared in the place where I was assigned to duty. Earlier than the preachers generally, I was out on the street, mounted, and inquiring the way to ———— ————. One gentleman said, "All I know about it is, they go south," pointing that way. Then it was good-by to the seat of the Conference, good-by to the few friends I saw, and turning the face of George, my faithful and only companion, southward, I moved off for the Gulf of Mexico, feeling assured that if I saw nobody on the way, I could find the place by coasting. I was glad I had brought all my necessary things with me; for to have gone after them would have cost me five hundred miles extra riding, and the station in which I was assigned to duty a loss of half a month's time. I attributed my good luck in this respect to the foresight and kindly advice of the good brother who told me to take all my things along, and meditated much that day upon what he laconically said: "*You do not know what is to become of you.*"

OBSERVATIONS ON THE WAY.

Of course the journey was not made without its share of novelty and incidents. For several days I traveled on horseback. The thing that struck me most forcibly was the deep solitude of pine forests. How strangely in contrast they were with the short, shrubby growth of the cross-woods skirting, and in some places edging far into the missions I had left! and how much in contrast with the wide, open prairies in which no forest grove of shrub or tree intercepts the vision, or interferes with the soft undulation of hill and vale which there we so often see! Upon the traveler unused to it, the deep, dark shades of thick, heavy pineries place a spirit of loneliness, and upon none perhaps more than upon one who has grown accustomed to the bright light of the expansive plains in the "far West."

Finally, however, I came to a place where it was necessary for me to change my mode of traveling. It was at a place generally called "the Bluff." It had a prefix to distinguish the generic term, but this was the local expression of it. When the skeptic with whom I lodged found my destination and business, he became very persistent in his persuasions that I did not need a horse down there, stating the great price I would have to give for corn, and that it would be very expensive to take him along. From all I gathered from him and other sources, I became convinced that it would not at all pay me to have a horse in the station where there was every convenience for "boating it" about. But how hard it was for me to consent to part with my faithful companion, whose service to me I could never reward! But by the force of circumstances, and with much regret, I resolved to part with a dumb creature between whom and myself there was the tenderest mutual attachment; and on account of this very thing, together with the services he rendered me, I have always cherished his memory with emotions of pleasure. I might here speak of a time when probably George and I might meet again, and in a renewal of our friendship find much mutual pleasure, but I have already given you the incident by which indulging thoughts and giving expression to them on this line resulted in evil—even the loss of a congregation. I therefore make no argument on that line. I shall only patiently wait and see the unmeasured developments that lie deeply hidden in the mind of *Him* "in whose hand is the soul of every living creature." There being no competition in buyers, I left my faithful horse in the hands of the skeptic with whom I lodged for the night, who, I had evidences to believe, notwithstanding, treated his horses with more kindness than many Christians. I received for him one hundred dollars, as I thought only two-thirds of his value.

Soon after parting with George, I got aboard a steam-boat, the Sunflower, Captain Clemmens commanding—a clever, genial officer; one who, so far as I could discover, respected God and his cause. On the way down, I found there was aboard a young minister, Brother A——. Though he did not go all the way, yet we had a pleasant time alternating between conversation and shooting at alligators. I remained aboard the Sunflower, and took breakfast on it next morning, it being late at night when I arrived at my station.

IMPRESSIONS OF THE PLACE.

Here I was, on one of the most beautiful mornings I ever saw, at my destination. My eyes fell upon things in strange contrast with all I had ever seen before. I heard no caroling of birds to tell me the light of day had come again; at least, if there were such things, I did not heed them. The music that saluted my ears on awaking was "old ocean in its roar"—a music as undying as the waters are existing, whose symphony never ceases day nor night. The morning was so beautiful and quiet that all alarming symptoms left my mind, and I began to feel a readiness to make myself known, and enter upon my duty in the place.

I stepped off the boat alone and "single-handed." Every face looked strange to me, and some were talking other than the English language. I looked at those passing here and there, as if judging human nature. Finally my eye struck my man and I hailed him. Said I: "Sir, do you know any preachers in this place?" "Yes," said he, "I know two, and I believe that is all; one is a Presbyterian and the other a Methodist." "Very good," said I, "and thank you. Will you please direct me to the Methodist minister's house?" This he did with care, and kindly. I therefore soon found myself at a place that felt like a home, and for which I devoutly thanked God. But this man was greatly afflicted. It was caused from exposure while traveling and preaching the word. The veins of his legs were so enlarged that he could not get about only by keeping them tightly laced with slips made for the purpose. This minister, however, was a great help to me in getting an introduction to the place.

There were here a battalion of cavalry encamped in barracks out southward of the city, if city it might be called, for it was a place of only a few hundred inhabitants. There was also a fort of earth-works below at the mouth of the harbor, and a few companies of soldiers with an armament of cannon and small arms. Lying off the harbor might be seen now and then a huge ship called "a blockader," watching for any craft that might be attempting either to pass out or to come in. The orange-trees were rich with their fruit, and the season of ripening was at hand. This beautiful yellow fruit looked invitingly as it hung in lovely contrast, intermixed with the deep green foliage of the trees that bore it. No fruit-bearing tree is more beautiful than the orange-tree at this season of the year. The soil had more the consistence of baked tar than any I ever saw. All cultivation was with the spade and hoe. There were no fields, only small garden-patches. In order to make these gardens more of a loose loam, they mixed in shells, ashes, and many other extraneous substances. It was not unusual to see garden soil held in by plank much elevated above the common level as it had from time to time been improved by mixing in other substances. Here were ships and smaller sea craft at anchor, seeming to hesitate as to what was best, but occasionally sailing out and taking the risk of capture.

First Sermon in the Station.

But by and by Sunday came, which was the second from the close of the Conference, and I was to occupy the pulpit. The pulpit, did I say? Yes, the pulpit. Why, I had never preached in a pulpit, and had seen but few of them since I had been licensed to preach. But the bell sounded, and the people and the new preacher were soon face to face—that is, as much so as the pulpit would allow, for it was rather a huge piece of architecture, unduly tall, with a column at each end a foot or two higher, to act as lamp-rest whenever there was need of lamps. These columns obstructed the vision in those quarters, and appeared to trouble me as I sat back a little restless, with scarcely from my eyebrows upward visible to my audience, and knowing that the columns would be above my shoulders when standing. The place and situation were in strange contrast with my former experience. My preaching was strictly after my own style, and the sermon, as I suppose, contained nothing odd in it, as nobody laughed, cried, or talked during the delivery of it. Just before dismissing the congregation, I recommended to their consideration the cutting off of those ungainly and troublesome columns on a plane with the book-board.

This awakened some smiles, pleasant or otherwise I could not at the time comprehend. It matters not to say what became of those columns, but all people do observe that such a fault in architecture is now corrected in all progressive places.

FISHING AND FISHERS.

As has been already observed, this was "a monstrous fishy place." The fish ordinarily taken with the seine was the mullet, which is a fish of small size but well flavored. The manner of seining is on this wise: Leaving one end held in the hands of the fishing party on shore, the seine is placed aboard a skiff. The skiff is then rowed off, dropping out the seine as it moves until it comes around in its circuit to shore again, with the other end of the seine near to the place of starting. The seine is held near to the surface by floats, and sinks by weights. Then comes the hardest labor attached to the business—drawing the seine to shore. This is done by the whole party on shore. Two or three skiffs go round to render any assistance that may be needed in case of its hanging. Sometimes a man has to leave his skiff and dive under to do the disentangling; but being accustomed to the water, he goes under without word or hesitation. One haul is all the party ever make, for they always get more fish than they want. They select the best, and put the others back into the water. The party being always on the water, and almost daily accustomed to such sights, do not appear enlivened, and to see sport in the business like Kentuckians and Tennesseans, but simply as any other business to get something to eat.

But there was another mode of fishing practiced here. It was the ordinary way practiced by Kentuckians on the creeks of that State—a line, sinker, and bait, but no pole. A bar of lead fastened to the line within a foot of the hook answered for a sinker, and an ounce of fresh beef for a bait—a *picket* or stake was driven in the ground, to which the end of the line was fastened, and the baited end was by a whirling motion thrown a hundred feet or more out into the strait. Then the fisherman only had to sit and wait and watch his line, which was never very long if it was a day for fish to bite, before he saw it beginning to move. The fisherman then, if awkward in the management of his game, sometimes got his hands sharply cut by the line. It was often no easy job, and required some skill, to successfully bring to shore from a distance of a hundred feet, holding to a small line, a fish weighing from six to forty pounds. The experience some had with the large ones made them wish that only the small ones would bite. The place of general fishing was a place of two banks; the first one broke off abruptly, and was about three feet above the other, which gradually sloped to the water's edge. The fish was in the end of the struggle first hauled by hook and line on this first gradually sloping bank. If a small one, then lifted in the same way to the upper bank; but if a heavy one, the fisherman went down to where it was, put his hands in its gills and threw it on the bank above. These fish never floundered like Kentucky minnows, but after their great struggle in the water, their energy appeared to be entirely broken down, and they quietly yielded themselves to their fate. The best time for fishing was either at the beginning of the ebbing or flowing of the tide. The kind of fish generally taken were red fish, fresh-water cat, or salt-water cat, according to the way the tide was moving. But the fisherman soon learns to draw in his tackle and go home, when a school of the porpoise come near. They are fishers themselves, and when they move about in numerous shoals, making now and then drumming sounds, the smaller fish getting intermixed with them become embarrassed and are taken. It is nothing unusual to see the smaller fish leaping out of the water when embarrassed in these schools.

There was another kind of fishing done here. The men who followed it were a weather-stained, dirty-looking class, who either did not know how or else had no heart to aspire above a little hut and a skiff as their full stock of property. They emphatically obtained daily their daily bread. How they managed on Sunday I did not learn. Whether like the children of Israel they got a double supply for one day in each week, I know not; but one thing is true, they had the liberty of the waters, and the oyster-reefs were free. By being out early you might see these oyster-men unlocking their skiffs and starting on their daily labor. Of course, each one in a skiff to himself, and in rowing always has his back toward the point of destination; yet he never looks to see, but makes his landing at the precise point he desires without ever looking once ahead. He is simply governed by the position and range of objects on shore. When once landed, then begins his work of loading, which is done with long-handled tongs of short grapple. One part of the long handle is pressed against his shoulder, the other is held stiffly in his hands; and thus standing in his skiff, he breaks the oysters loose from their reef and lifts them with the same implement into the skiff. When loaded, with the same precision and skill he comes again to shore, and immediately begins the work of opening the shells, which is in some respects done after the fashion of a Kentucky boy out with his little bucket gathering berries—he will now and then slip one into his mouth. So this oyster-man, who no doubt is hungry by this time, as he opens the shells divides between his bucket and mouth. But when the work is finished, which is generally toward the close of day, he again locks his skiff to shore, and starts for his little hut, where wife and children are waiting for his daily earnings; but he goes by a trading-shop and exchanges his oysters for family supplies such as his judgment teaches him to get. Here I learned to love oysters, but never took any stock in this kind of fishing.

Hon. William L. Yancey.

While here, I witnessed the return to our country of the Hon. Wm. L. Yancey, who had been sent early in the war between the States to the court of St. James as an agent of the Confederate Government. The manner of his return fully illustrated the extremity of the South even at that time. The ports were all blockaded, and it was just now and then a vessel could slip in or out. This gentleman exercised the precaution necessary to make it safely back to his native land. He came in aboard the schooner Stingeray on one of the stormiest evenings I ever saw. He came by way of Cuba, and of course practically in disguise. He represented the British Government as stoical on Southern recognition; that the government was exceedingly politic, and had great patience to wait and see; that the English people were not at all affected by the cry that "cotton is king;" that in his opinion the English Government would never recognize the Southern Confederacy until they became greatly changed in sentiment. He did not speak at all encouragingly of the matter. He appeared to be exceedingly open in all his statements in reference to the policy and intentions of the English Government, and left the impression that we were in the struggle, and must unaided and with but little sympathy fight our own battle.

Wm. L. Yancey was exceedingly Southern—a man of strong convictions and of very decided character. You did not have to thump him and sound him to get at his principles. They stood prominently to view like the strongly written features of his face. Though a little wanting in conservatism, yet he was as pious in his intentions and as philosophic in thought as the effeminate statesman who gradually, for want of courage to defend, compromises away his country's liberty under the authority of statute law. However much people may differ, there is something to admire in the character of such a man as he was. Whatever cause he espoused, he never uttered a word nor did an act that weakened it.

Anchored in a Lake.

Having had the liberty of so large a territory on the missions just previous to this station work, I felt a little oppressively the confinement. I was invited to visit and preach in a couple of little towns above, distant about thirty-five or forty miles. I concluded to go under the invitation, inasmuch as for some cause neither one just in those times had any preaching in regular order. A lake of water twenty-five miles in diameter lay between my station and those towns, and in order to reach them had to be crossed. This was done variously, either in small sailing vessels or by steam-boats. I went up to one of these towns on a small sailing vessel, and had a pleasant voyage. When I got ready to return, the only vessel that was at hand was the smallest steam-boat I ever saw, called The Dime. I took passage aboard this little *craft,* and was soon on my return voyage. Every thing went well enough until we had got far out into the lake, when the little *animal* which I was riding was found to be pitching at a furious rate—up and over again, not very unlike some of the mustangs used to do me in the West when they wished to unlade before I had steered them into port. "What is this, captain?" said I. "A gale, sir," answered he. "What is that you have down there?" "Cast anchor, sir." "Why don't you go on and get out of the storm?" "Can't make any headway, sir." "Then, why do you not turn round and go back?" "It would be dangerous not to keep the bow to the wind and tide, sir." Here I hesitated, thought of Jonah, and wondered. The little *animal, lariated* in the middle of the lake, kept its face full fronting the gale and tide, would rear up and go over every surge of the water seemingly as stately as a time-moving pendulum. The captain told me that it would be very dangerous if the rope that held it should break. Of course I knew all about the running, braying, pitching, and capering of a mustang when the picket pulled up or the lariat broke.

"Captain, how long since you were caught out this way?" "This is my first time, sir." "How long have you been navigating this water?" "Twenty-five years." "Do you know any captain that has been caught this way?" "Not exactly, sir." Just then I looked down the boat, and saw by its motion of riding the waves that it was limber, a thing I had never noticed in any steam-boat. Said I, rather anxiously: "Captain, did you know your boat is limber?" He looked and saw it springing and bending as it rode the waves, and remarked with little concern: "Steam-boats are not built like ships, stayed with masts and ropes, but all of them are limber." It was now about midday. Said I, again: "How long do you think this gale will last?" "I think it will all be over by to-morrow," said he. "Do you think your boat can stand it until to-morrow?" "I think so, if it don't get any worse." "But if it breaks in two?" said I, lamentingly. "Then we will hold to the pieces," said he.

This was enough. I was the only passenger aboard. I retired to my berth thinking of this brave captain, who seemed to be as much composed as if no gale had struck and troubled his little craft. The gale continued, and all the motions of the vessel, until just twelve o'clock at night, when the rain began to beat heavily and to pour down as a flood. It seemed that the waters of another lake had been raised and were pouring down again in this. Lightning flashes were seen, but no note of thunder was heard above the general roar. The little boat on which we rode rose, plunged, and struggled for its position like a brave warrior in furious combat. In the pitchy darkness of the night I could not see how much it was bending. I was now fully impressed it would bear through; for if it had intended to come to pieces, it would have done so long ago. When the storm lulled and the waves became broken, it did appear that the little thing would shake itself to pieces. It acted like a thing in full muscular exercise, without a nerve-power to give it regular motion. There we staid until day-dawn. About nine o'clock in the morning, under a beautiful sky, as though nothing unusual had occurred, with a gladsome heart, and I reckon with a pleasant smile, I rode the little animal still alive into the port of my station. I conclude by saying I felt very morally inclined.

14

My Last Days in the Station.

From the first it was evident to my mind that the station work would not be pleasant to me. To go with a mission and yet not be able to carry it out, because the minds of the people were diverted to the war which had now commenced in great earnestness, tended in a great degree to keep me uncomfortable. The war was the all-absorbing topic, and the signs of it were visible all around my little station. Blockaders were almost continuously in sight. The people were in dread that their little city would be taken. Vessels were occasionally slipping in and out, and sometimes one run down and captured, in full open view of the city. The smoke of the cannon and the vertical spray of the shot falling on the water were plainly visible, as well as the hearing of the booming roar. It was war, war, and the people's minds and hearts were fixed in it in a great degree to the neglect of the proper worship of God.

I turned my attention partly to preaching to the soldiers. They listened well, and many of them were Christians. I enjoyed their society. They were out on the front, but appeared less excited on the great question at issue than the common people. They presented none of the appearance of a piece of working machinery so much as they did the great fact that each one was a machine within himself, acting on the broad ground of the principle involved.

I left and went to the war. This begins a new line of thought, because it was a new line of operation. But now, dear mother, I know you are weary and must have rest. We shall have to take another evening to finish our report.

But tell me what stranger that is in the other room, whom I could see through the window, and who appeared to be so busy writing all the time of my narration.

Mother: "Why, that is our short-hand reporter."

Author: "What has he been writing so much?"

Mother: "He has taken down your narrative for me."

Author: "What do you want with it?"

Mother: "Why, I am going to publish it."

Author: "Why, is it so you are still prankish as in the days when you were my young mother and I your little boy at your knee? Has time not changed you even in this?"

Mother: "It has all been prearranged, for we knew you would tell us something we want to keep; and it shall be fairly done, with such revisal as may be needed."

THE END.

www.ingramcontent.com/pod-product-compliance
Lightning Source LLC
Chambersburg PA
CBHW020832230426
43666CB00007B/1195